THE CONFEDERATE

by
William M. Bobo
"A South Carolinian"

THE CONFEDERATE
REPRINT COMPANY
☆   ☆   ☆   ☆
WWW.CONFEDERATEREPRINT.COM

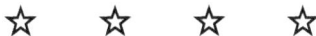

The Confederate
by William M. Bobo

Originally Published in 1863
by S. H. Goetzel and Company
Mobile, Alabama

Reprint Edition © 2014
The Confederate Reprint Company
Post Office Box 2027
Toccoa, Georgia 30577
www.confederatereprint.com

Cover and Interior by
Magnolia Graphic Design
www.magnoliagraphicdesign.com

ISBN-13: 978-0692307397
ISBN-10: 0692307397

CHAPTER ONE

☆ ☆ ☆ ☆

The wisest, purest, and best of all the men this continent has given to the world, left us, in his farewell message of instruction, some counsels of inestimable value, which, if followed by the Nation, would have rendered the disruption of the old Union, which, however, no one can regret less than myself, unnecessary; and the United States might have moved on in peace and prosperity for ages. This separation would have been unnecessary, because the causes which led to, and justified it, would not have been allowed to spring into existence, if the maxims and admonitions of Washington had been heeded by the bigoted fanatics of the North. The Yankee race, true descendants of their false and fanatical progenitors, the bigoted Pilgrim Fathers, by their unceasing envy, hatred, jealousy and all uncharitableness towards the South, and their egotism, self-righteousness, dissimulation, cunning, cupidity and hypocrisy, have caused the severance of that union between the States which can never be renewed.

The system of intriguing, selfish class legislation, and unscrupulous over-reaching, in all things, all with whom they came in contact, was inaugurated by the Yankees of the North in the earliest years of the United States Government, and was steadily, perseveringly and unscrupulously pursued for more than three quarters of a century, when it culminated in the election of Abraham Lincoln as President of the United States, on avowed local, partisan and fanatical principles. This caused the cup of the South, already filled with wrongs, injuries, outrages and insults, to overflow. The Union, once so loved but now so prostituted and debased, was spurned with contempt and loathing. The several States now composing the Confederacy, each withdrew from that defiled and defiling Union; avowed their determination no longer to be a part of the once honored, but now degraded United States; in their sovereign capacities they formed a confederation amongst themselves, and quietly — unfortunately far too quietly — awaited the result. The result was war, as I, for one, never for a moment doubted. The question of peace or war was answered on the 12th of April, now nearly two years ago, by the guns of South Carolina at Fort Sumter.

The bombardment and reduction of Fort Sumter, forced upon the South by the shuffling, duplicity, falsehood, and finally the plain and palpable treachery of the Northern Government, inaugurated a war which still continues, and the end and result of which no human wisdom can foretell. Swelling rapidly into vast proportions, such as no country has seen for generations, that war now employs the time and occupies the energies of, probably, nearly two millions of men. The pecuniary character of this war is no less astonishing, no less stupendous, than its military phase. The Abolition Government, by its own admission, has been, for over one year, and still is squandering money at the fabulous rate at over three millions a day, or nearly one thousand millions per annum. Our own force in the field, and our own expenditure, though very far below that of our Abolition foes, is very great, and would, under any ordinary circumstances, be considered enormous.

This war has now continued nearly two years, and it seems improbable, in the nature of things, that it should continue very much longer. Be this as it may, there is already much speculation, North and South, as well as in Europe, as to the conclusion of this devastating strife, which, in the wide area of its actions and consequences, is visiting suffering and privation upon multitudes of the distant inhabitants of Europe, as well as upon the belligerents themselves. Speculations as to foreign intervention are rife; propositions for a general convention of all the original States, e're the dissolution, with New Jersey as an arbiter, have been thrown out by Governor Seymour, of New York, in his first message, and letter writers and editors in Abolitiondom are occupied in giving out suggestions, and devising means for bringing this sanguinary struggle to an end.

One of the maxims of the "Father of his Country," the wisdom of which is patent to all, is, "In time of peace prepare for war." At this time I deem the converse of the maxim worthy of serious attention — "In time of war prepare for peace."

This, under any circumstances, would be a point of importance, but in the present state of our affairs – in view of the causes which precipitated this war, the character of those who wage it against us, the manner in which they have carried it on, the avowed end they have in view, and the tremendous stake (no less than liberty or slavery to a vile, fanatical, and vandal horde), which we have in the issue – render it one of primary and vital importance. That this war, like all other wars, must have an end – that peace must eventually come – is clear in the nature of things – is the plain dictate of ordinary common sense – is proved by all past experience, as recorded in the pages of history. Such being clearly the necessary finale of this tremendous struggle, is it not advisable, even now, to consider, and reflect, and meditate well what shall be the nature and character of that peace? What shall be the terms of such peace? What is necessary to give us present indemnity and future security? What is due to the honor and dignity of the Confederate Government, and what amends shall be demanded from the Abolition Government for all its wrongs, indignities and outrages? Taking it for granted that no one of true Southern blood or feeling can, for a moment, doubt the ultimate triumph of the Confederate States – and that, however outnumbered in men or surpassed in the means and appliances of war, victory must eventually perch upon our banner, it appears to be a not inappropriate season for considering what use we shall make of that victory to which we look forward with unwavering confidence, from the tried valor of our gallant soldiery and the approval of benignant Heaven. The ultimate success of our cause is beyond a question. Six millions of people, united as we are, occupying a territory extensive as ours, trained to arms from boyhood, bold, hardy, active and chivalrous, never, have been subjugated in the world's annals. What though the enemy be three, or five – what though they were ten to one? The result would still be the same. Fighting for our altars and our firesides, for all that is prized by, and all that is dear to man, we would meet the insolent invaders, the bigots, the robbers, the ruffians, at every point, and drive back their shattered and bleeding ranks in terror and disgrace.

This has been already shown on many a bloody field of battle. Not two years of the war have elapsed, but time and again our gallant troops have met the foe – met them on their own chosen fields – met them armed and equipped with the most approved weapons and the choicest accessories of modern war and modern art, and ourselves indifferently armed, badly clothed, and but partially organized and disciplined – and have conquered them when they outnumbered us two, and three, and even four to one. True, the successes have not all been ours. The many advantages of the enemy, and, perhaps, too much confidence or too little prudence on our part, have caused us some serious and sad reverses. But the general balance of events, since the war began, is greatly in our favor. At the end of nearly two years, we are stronger in every respect than at any preceding period, and to-day better prepared to cope with the enemy, than at any time since the commencement of hostilities.

Thus far all the efforts of the Abolitionists to cripple us in our resources, and to "crush out the rebellion," have signally failed. Despite their blockade, we have more and better arms than we have ever had before, and ample supplies of ammunition and military stores. Despite their several "Ons to Richmond!" Richmond is still ours, and they are, perhaps, further than ever either from gaining possession of Richmond or "crushing out the rebellion in thirty, sixty or ninety days." Our enemies, like the apostles of Millerism (a fanaticism of their own fabrication), have been obliged to change their figures. What time they may now give themselves to accomplish their arduous labors it is impossible to say. One thing is certain; they will again fail ignominiously. A united people, fighting for their homes, upon their own soil, are not to be subdued, and the superior race is never conquered by the inferior.

The Southron, descended from the Cavaliers of Europe, is of the superior race. Accustomed from his youth to the saddle and the rifle, he may be said to be born a soldier.

The Abolitionist of the North, sprung from the scum of England, of Scotland and of Ireland, bred in bigotry and intolerance, is of the inferior race. Accustomed from infancy to the last, the needle, the axe or the yardstick, to thrift, fraud and chicane, having, in most cases, never mounted a horse or fired a gun in his whole life, he may be safely said to have been born not a soldier. These, with the addition of ignorant and pauper foreigners, the Hessians of this war, constitute the forces of our enemy.

The motives which actuate us are higher, purer, nobler than those of the enemy, in much the same degree that we are morally and personally superior to them. Their incentives to battle are conquest, plunder, revenge; ours, religion, home, family, liberty. In such a struggle, I repeat it, the better cause and the superior race, with the favor of Heaven, already so remarkably manifested in our behalf, never can be subjugated. The struggle may still be protracted, desperate and desolating. Our privations and sufferings may continue, and even increase; our best blood may yet flow more profusely than heretofore, but victory and independence are certain.

From State to State, from county to county, from hill to plain, on mountain and by river, we will meet the enemy, and we will conquer them.

If defeated in one field, it shall only restring our nerves and fortify our resolution to win the next one. If, unhappily broken and dispersed, we will carry on the guerrilla warfare, man to man, whenever and wherever we may meet a foe. From every hill and hollow, from every tree and thicket, the sudden fire of death shall flash in the face of the enemy. If unable to cope with the ruthless foe in masses, we will cut them off in detail, and by all and any means, until our outraged land is free from their pollution. Their patrols, pickets, sentinels, scouting parties, shall be picked off by the unerring rifle; their communications broken up, and their trains captured and destroyed. The war shall be by day and by night, and the conflict unceasing, until the Abolition horde shall be glad to escape, if escape they can, with barely life, from the land they so boastfully came to conquer and possess. They shall be attacked, wearied, harassed, destroyed, at all times, in all ways and all places, until we shall

> Make our valleys, reeking caves,
> Live in the awe-struck minds of men;
> Till bigots tremble, when the knaves
> Mention each bloody Southern glen.[1]

---

1. Slightly altered from the original.

CHAPTER TWO

☆ ☆ ☆ ☆

If there was a bag of coffee in hell,
a Yankee would go after it!

The above forcible, though not very elegant quotation, expresses well the sense entertained by its author of the great principle of all Yankeedom – immeasurable avarice. The remark is attributed to the black Christopho, once the nominal President of the quasi Republic of Hayti. It comes from one who had ample opportunity for observing the unfathomable baseness of Yankee character, as displayed in the West Indies, far from home and unrestrained by the factitious rules of their society, or the fictitious curbs of their peculiar home-morality. The authority, I admit, is not a very respectable one, and I should never have dreamed of quoting it against a gentleman or a respectable people; but applied to the Yankees, coming from one of that race they profess to consider their equals, and in whose welfare they profess so warm an interest, it seems peculiarly just and appropriate.

It is this unprincipled and most unscrupulous people with which we are now in conflict.

In order that we may justly appreciate the true character of our Yankee foes, it is necessary to look a little into their antecedents, and see what record they have left upon the pages of history; for they, too, like plague, pestilence and famine, the Simoom, the tempest, and the earthquake, and other scourges of humanity, have a history – a history filled with the outrages they have committed upon society, and written in the tears of their helpless and hapless victims.

Rising into influence and power by their characteristic mendacity and hypocrisy, in the seventeenth century – floating, like other scum, to the top of the cauldron of revolution – for the sins of mankind, probably, certainly for their sorrow, and to their own eternal disgrace and infamy, they seized upon the powers, and wielded (for a brief period, by the blessing of God) the destinies of a nation. Professing, a desire to reform the Government and restrain the King, they destroyed the Government and murdered the King. Pretending to reform the Church and purify religion, they overthrew the Church and destroyed religion.

I am no apologist for the Stuarts; I am no zealous advocate of the Church of England. Both, no doubt, had their foibles and their faults. But when a king, in many respects worthy of all consideration, and certainly a gentleman and a Christian, is assassinated in cold blood, by a wild band of low, unprincipled, and shameless robbers and villains; when a church, venerable from its antiquity, the sublime beauty of its service, the pure character, fervid piety, and deep learning of nearly every one of its highest officials, and the unexceptional lives and faithful labors of the vast majority of its subordinate priesthood, is overthrown, shattered, trampled in the dust by a grovelling, vicious, ignorant rabble, we cannot forbear the expression of sincere sympathy with the one, nor our just detestation of and deep abhorrence of the other.

It is no pleasant task to review the history of the "Puritans," the "Pilgrims," as they are wont to style themselves. A career of such ruthless selfishness, of such unprincipled conduct, of such hypocritical profession, it is impossible to find in the records of any other people. It is not pleasant to unmask hypocrisy, to expose villainy, to unveil vice in all its deformity. It is disagreeable to see human nature thus degraded. It wounds our self-respect to think we are of the same human family. Yet such is the task imposed on one who gives even a brief sketch of the lives of the "Puritans," and their undoubted descendants, the "Yankees." It is not easy to impart a correct idea of these people to the Southern mind. For more than half a century, Southern apathy has permitted our country to be deluged with Northern books and Northern papers. Our school books, our histories, our journals, even our almanacs, have been written, printed, published, by Northern men in Northern cities. To justify their own rascality and the villainy of their progenitors, these Yankee writers have misstated facts, perverted the Bible and falsified history. They have even changed the vices and crimes of their forefathers into virtues and heroic actions. They claim, and with unabashed boldness, with brazen impudence, still claim for those selfish impostors the crown and the praise of martyrs and heroes.

Every page of true history falsifies this infamous and impudent claim. But how is true history to be obtained? Fortunately, Truth is immortal! The true records of the infamous career of the vile sect, of which our vandal enemies, the Yankees, are the legitimate descendants and the true and faithful representatives, still exist and can be procured, despite all their mighty and persevering efforts, during more than two centuries, to hide them under mountains of falsehood and misrepresentation.

The Yankee Abolitionists declare that "the Pilgrim Fathers fled from persecution in England, and came, self banished, noble, heroic martyrs, to the desert wilds of the New World to escape from that persecution which they were unable to resist, and to enjoy the inestimable privilege of worshipping God according to the dictates of their own conscience." *Vide* Peter Parley, Abbott, and every Geography and History, and almost every other schoolbook, published in Yankeedom for the last half century.

These assertions, if well substantiated, might give to the Puritans a claim to some small credit, but by no means to any part of the glory claimed for them by their posterity. They would be entitled to that praise, whatever it may be worth, which is due to those who prefer to abandon their country rather than boldly resist tyranny, and choose to expatriate themselves rather than incur the risk of winning the crown of martyrdom! But not content to permit these cowardly runagates to sink quietly into that oblivion which their insignificance so well deserved, even if the story so industriously manufactured by their descendants were true, they must needs, forsooth, be elevated to the dignity of patriots, heroes, martyrs! Was such unblushing impudence ever heard or seen before? Truly is the son worthy of the sire! The Yankee does credit to the Puritan!

But so far is the Yankee story of the Puritans from being true, it is absolutely and entirely false. In whole and in part; in the aggregate and in the constituents, the whole of this Yankee fable, this Puritan apotheosis, is, in every essential point, not only wholly untrue, but the very reverse of truth.

Take any Yankee history of the Puritans; change every affirmation to a negation, and every negation to an affirmation, and the work would approximate far more nearly to that great constituent, the absence of which destroys entirely the value of all history – Truth.

The true history of the Puritans is, in substance and briefly, as follows:

During the revolutionary periods in England in the time of Charles I., the bigots and fanatics, of which that distracted period was so painfully prolific, banded their hitherto disjointed forces into one or more parties, and in the hope of power, vengeance for fancied wrongs, and the spoils to be reaped by the plunder of the rich in the anarchy and confusion of a revolution, united against the Throne and the Church. Upon the overthrow of the Throne and the downfall of the Church, first one faction and then another of these unprincipled schemers obtained possession of the chief powers of the Government. Finally all the powers of the Government, civil and religious, fell into the hands of the Independents, the real Puritans, with Cromwell at their head. Behold, then, these Purists in religion and politics, these pious and zealous reformers, these self-styled saints, wielding for a time the whole power of the English Empire! And in what manner did they use the power which they had so surreptitiously and criminally obtained! Truly, the spectacle is curious – painful but instructive. The king they had professed to desire only to confine within the constitutional limits of his prerogative, their leaders – who had neither conquered nor captured him – bought with money from the Scots, his native subjects, to whom, in confidence of their good faith, he had nobly surrendered his person and his safety. The Scots –

not the nation, but the Puritans amongst them, who held the balance of power – basely sold him to his blood-thirsty enemies; thus sharing the guilt and infamy of this unsurpassedly infamous bargain of blood. The Puritans, true to their character, their nature, and their instincts, immediately butchered the king. In the case of the Church, these blood-thirsty saints acted with equal consistency and equal infamy. The Church was overthrown, its ministers robbed and banished, its property plundered and destroyed. For the Church they substituted the Conventicle, for the regularly ordained priesthood, any crazy or intriguing fanatics who fancied they had "had a call;" for the religion hallowed by centuries, their own wild, crude and frantic sectarian doctrines; for the pure morals of the Bible, a still, starched, fanatical, gloomy morality, which proscribed any exhibition of feelings, however innocent and noble, and all manifestations of affection, however natural and sacred.

Pretending to be the very saints of the earth, and entirely separate and distinct from all others, whom they designated as Gentiles, world's people, and malignants, they endeavored to mark the distinction by manners the most frigid and formal; by hair of formal cut, by habiliments of sober style and sombre hue, by long faces and longer prayers. Even in ordinary conversation, abandoning the common language of common sense, they adopted a jargon mixed up of constant random, irreverent quotations of the obsolete expressions of Holy Writ, and their own sectarian cant, which would have been supremely absurd and ludicrous, had it not been at the same time wicked and impious. All the usual courtesies and amenities of social life were forbidden; amusements the most innocent prohibited; customs, fetes, holidays the most sacred from time

and association, denounced, and every usage, amusement
or indulgence which could console or cheer the heart of
man, discarded. Even the ordinary sounds of the human
voice were objectionable in the view of these new Pharisees, and a low, halting, hesitating, hoarse and snuffling
through the nose, became the chosen tone of the Elect.

Such is the character and such the conduct of the
Puritans in England during the day of their power. They
seemed to think the only conduct pleasing to God was that
which was most unnatural and revolting to man; that the
only sure road to salvation was that which overran and
trod down all the natural affections; in short, that the only
way to Heaven was to make earth as nearly as possible a
Hell.

In the madness of their blind and furious zealotry,
they tore down the cross from the churches, although,
with characteristic ignorance and inconsistency, they
sometimes allowed the mitre to remain, leaving intact the
emblem of rank of the priest, while they impiously trampled on that of his, and, according to their professions,
their God – the sign and banner of a common hope and a
common salvation. They banished the Bible from their
pulpits, because it was read in the churches. Though
kneeling in prayer is enjoined, they determined to pray
standing, for the reason that churchmen kneel. In all things
they endeavored to be as unlike Christians as possible –
and they succeeded; there were none like them before,
there are none others like them now; may there be no
more like them forever!

Incapable, from the very coarseness and baseness
of their nature, of appreciating harmony, they banished all
decent music and all tolerable tunes from their places of
worship, and adopted a mode and manner of singing, at

their places of worship, which has been the abhorrence and ridicule of all succeeding time. Ignorant of all that adorns, elevates, soothes, and gives a charm to life, they made vandal war upon the fine arts. They broke down the altars, shattered the windows, overthrew the statues, and destroyed the paintings found either in the churches or in private habitations. Even the last resting place of the dead was no more sacred in their eyes than it is in the eyes of their Yankee successors. They broke open the tombs and defaced the sepulchres. As there are no bounds to fanaticism except those imposed by force, the Puritans continued madly in their wild career, from one outrage, from one absurdity, from one monstrosity, to another more outrageous, more absurd and more monstrous still. Finally, abjuring all laws except those of the Bible, as interpreted by themselves, and denying all authority on earth except that of Jesus Christ, they were ready to make war upon all law, all rulers and all authority; and would, inevitably, have thrown everything sacred or civil, into one common anarchy. But this did not suit the views of their leader. Cromwell, the only man of marked genius their party ever produced, had used them for his own purposes, and through their aid he had reached the great object of his mighty ambition. He had no further use for them. He was in possession of supreme power; they could give him no more. This last phase of their party, the rise of the "Fifth Monarchy" faction, threatened even to endanger the stability of his power. True to himself, but false to them, as they were to all the world, he determined to destroy them, and he succeeded without difficulty. Taking a few of disarmed guards, he drove the small remaining fragment of the "Rump" from the Parliament House, locked the door, and put the key in his pocket. He told them: "The Lord is tired of you!" Cromwell certainly was tired of them. Thenceforth he ruled England; ruled it absolutely – ruled it in the main wisely and well – but he ruled alone. The Puritan power was gone forever.

The nation had long been tired of them, and witnessed their overthrow and disgrace with joy.

On the death of Cromwell, there was much danger of anarchy. Then once more "the Saints," that is, the Puritans, made their appearance on the stage. They who had ruled the nation in madness; who had gone about with the word of God on their lips, and the sword of God in their hands; who had bound kings in chains, and nobles with links of iron, came forth from their hiding places to make one more desperate effort for power, one final struggle for empire.

But their day had gone by; their time had passed away.

Charles II. was recalled from his exile, and restored to the throne of his ancestors, amidst the wildest outbursts of loyalty and devotion. During his whole reign, careless, despotic, variable as it was – extravagant, vicious, and licentious as were his conduct and his court – the nation gladly submitted to his authority, and were content to overlook his foibles and his faults. They remembered the reign of "the Saints" – they had not forgotten when that iron rule of bigotry and intolerance weighed upon them like an Incubus, paralyzing, blighting, destroying everything pleasant and loveable in life, everything honorable, and elevating, and sacred in human nature. Then and there closed the history of Puritanism in England. Its power to do evil was gone. The Puritans, as a political power, then perished forever. In Europe they are heard of no more, and the very name itself would, long since, have sunk into merited oblivion, but that, while in power, it had shocked the world with an exhibition of follies, vices and crimes, which have doomed the name of Puritan to a most unenviable immortality.

So ends the history of the Puritans in the Old World. In my next number I purpose to give a brief history of its commencement and progress in the New.

CHAPTER THREE

☆　☆　☆　☆

In my last number I had finished my brief sketch of the history of the Puritans in the Old World. We have there seen them, after a most wild and wicked, though brief career, sink into merited insignificance and contempt. In the meantime, however, a portion of the same worthless faction had effected a lodgement on the shores of the New World.

In 1620, that unhappy ship, the *Mayflower*, had, unhappily for humanity, and doubly unhappily for us, disgorged upon the shores of America its fanatical crew, the spawn of that vile faction whose history I have already recorded, in the last number; whose principles, or rather total want of principles, I have portrayed; the progenitors of that infamous and beastly race whose fitting ruler is the "Ape Lincoln," and whose living incarnation is the "Beast Butler." These vile fanatics, with the false cry of persecution against themselves by the Church of England, and the true principles of persecution against everyone else in their hearts – principles which they very speedily put into practice – had just arrived from Europe.

It is of this portion of the Puritan clan I now pur- pose to write. I will mention here that I use the words, Puritan, Pilgrim Fathers, and Yankee, in common. They are almost convertible terms, and signify the same worth- less crew, whether in Europe or America. But it is of these – the *Mayflower* Puritans, the Pilgrim Fathers – I now intend to treat.

They are the Puritans for whom, especially, the lying Yankee writers have put forth such astonishing claims to respect and veneration. It is in their favor that the assertion is so emphatically made that "they fled from persecution on account of their religion, in England, to seek religious freedom in America." A claim more entirely unfounded, more utterly false, has seldom, if ever, been made by man. I have just said they arrived from Europe. I said it advisedly; they had come from Europe, but not from England, in the sense which their apologists and eu- logists mean to convey. The band who came over in the *Mayflower* (alas! why did she not sink on the way!) had been, for ten years, settled in Holland, and landed in Eng- land only to make the final arrangements for their emigra- tion to this continent. This is a notable specimen of the Yankee science of lying; it conveys a falsehood in the words of truth. They did sail from England, it is true, but they had first sailed from Holland, where they had lived for ten years just preceding their exodus. The idea con- veyed, and intended to be conveyed, by the Yankee writers, is that the severity of persecution in England drove the Pilgrim Fathers out of the country into the wilds of the New World, and that they sailed immediately from England, the place where they were persecuted, to avoid that persecution. To have stated the whole truth would have been to have belied the pretension to persecution. It would then have read, truly, but very absurdly, thus: "The Puritans fled from England, where they had not resided for the ten preceding years, to avoid persecution!" How could England have persecuted them when they were in Holland? This very natural question would have occurred to every reader. With ready skill in their favorite avocation, lying, the Yankee writers omit a very material fact in their statement, which would wholly disprove their charge of persecution, and then boldly present their false assertion to their readers. But perhaps they may say that the crew of the *Mayflower* were originally from England and that they were driven to Holland by persecution at home; and that, after all, the statement is substantially true. Let us see how this matter stands:

That the Pilgrims were originally from England is true; it is true, also, that it is said they fled to Holland to escape from persecution at home. But how is the fact? That persecution has prevailed in England, far too often for the credit of human nature, is unhappily too true. Each sect of religion, whenever in power, in that country, has persecuted all who differed with them in religious faith; and by no sect was persecution indulged in more freely than by the Puritans themselves during their brief period of power. But that they were suffering anything from persecution at the time of their emigration to Holland is entirely untrue.

This baseless slander of the Church and Government of England is of modern manufacture. This charge of persecution, entirely unfounded, and a vile fabrication, was not made by the emigrants to Holland themselves, nor any such pretence set up at the time. This, although perfectly characteristic, both of themselves and their successors, was too notoriously untrue, and too easily disproved, for them, brazen as they were, to dare the accusation. This task was reserved for their shameless descendants, at a distance of three thousand miles from the scene of action, and after the lapse of more than a century.

The only complaint the emigrants to Holland ever made was that "they were obliged to pay tithes for the support of a church in which they did not believe, and at whose altars they did not worship." This, which at any time and under any circumstances, could only have been considered a hardship, or an oppression, they never dared to exaggerate into persecution; this congenial labor has been gratuitously performed by their posterity.

It is plain, then, there was no persecution to drive the Puritans to Holland. But was taxation, or tithes to support the established church, although they did not believe in it, an oppression, or even a hardship in their case? "Circumstances," says the homely proverb, "alter cases." What were the circumstances in this case? Here I shall have to reproduce a little true history, which conflicts sadly with the false Yankee history of Puritanism. In the latter half of the eleventh century, William of Normandy conquered England, and assumed the crown of that country, which his descendants have held ever since, and, in the person of Queen Victoria, still hold. By a maxim of the English law, the highest title to all the land in the empire, fee simple, as well as the right of eminent domain, is vested in the crown. William the Conqueror being, by his conquest of England, the owner of all the land of the kingdom, partitioned it all into manors, as is recorded in Domesday Book (a work still extant), and conferred these manors upon his favorite chieftains, in reward for their services, but upon certain specific conditions.

This division of the land of England was made in

feudal times, and during the supremacy of the Roman Catholic Church. The principal conditions of the grants of these manors were the performance of the usual duties of feudatories, by those to whom the land was given, to their sovereign, and the payment of tithes for the support of the Church. In every other respect these grants of lands were pure benefactions – free gifts – the titles in fee to the grantees, and to their legal heirs, forever. The corresponding duties, on the part of the grantees, of feudal service to the grantor, and his successors in office, and the payment of tithes to the Church, were never, in any case, omitted, but were always expressly stipulated.

The Great Barons of the Conqueror subdivided those manors amongst their favorites, and they again amongst theirs, almost *ad infinitum*. Thus were the lands of England parcelled out, in every imaginable quantity, from the manor of the Great Baron, with its thousands of acres, to the small freehold of the laborer, of a few acres or even the fraction of an acre; but all held on the same specified terms, and all were subject to feudal services and Church rates, precisely as in the case of the original grantee, the Great Baron of the Conqueror. Thus, then, were all the lands of England held in possession of those who occupied them as a free gift, but upon very easy conditions, which gratitude would impel, and honesty would require the donee to fulfill. The Reformation, in the reign of Henry VIII., did not, in any way, alter these conditions, or the obligations of the holders of lands, any more than did the succession of one king to another. The death of one king, and the crowning of another, in no wise released the landholders from their duty of feudal service, and the overthrow of the Church of Rome, and the installation, in its place, of the Church of England, in no manner released them from the duty of paying tithes for the support of the Church. The feudal service, in the first cast, due to one king, became due to another, his successor. The obligation of paying tithes, in the other case, to one church, became binding upon the landholders to pay them to another church, its successor. And this duty, in the latter case, was it made clear and indisputable by the will of the king and the laws of the land.

We are now in a position to examine into the case of the Puritans, and their objections to paying tithes. If they possessed no lands, then they were not required to pay tithes; if they did possess lands, the question is, how did they come into that possession? Lands are neither made nor found. They pass by inheritance, by gift, or by purchase. In this country, where property in land passes wholly unencumbered, in ordinary cases, by any conditions whatever; where the title has been obtained by the labor, the energy, or the perseverance of the immediate holder, or of his predecessor; to require the owner to pay taxes for the support of a religion he did not believe in, might well be considered a hardship, and the enforced collection of those taxes might very properly be considered an op-pression; but is the case of the Puritans of England, in any respect, analogous?

By no means. If they held their lands by direct de-scent, they held them from those to whom they had been given upon the express condition that they should pay tithes for the support of the Church. In no possible way could they have avoided this stipulation, for if the lands were given to them, or had been purchased by them, they had been accepted, or had been purchased, subject to this well known condition. If they had been ignorant of this condition, it would have been their own fault, for it is the duty of every man who comes into the possession of land to ascertain the full nature of his title, and the duties which such possession may devolve upon him. But they were not ignorant of the condition. Every foot of land in England was held subject to the same condition, and the act was patent to all the world, at least all the English world. The effort, then, of the English Puritans to avoid the payment of tithes, instead of being the upright scruple of a sensitive conscience, as has been so speciously represented, was, in fact, a fraudulent attempt to commit a dishonest action – for it was an effort to avoid the payment of a just debt, and one which they knew to be just! How well do we recognize the real character of Puritanism here, and how, at all times, in all places, and under all circumstances, it is always true to itself, and to all its own low and grovelling instincts! The pretended scruple of a tender conscience was merely a knavish attempt to avoid the payment of a just debt. How worthy are their Yankee descendants of so immaculate an ancestry! The terribly persecuting Church and Government of England allowed, however, these poor, innocent and suffering martyrs, to sell all their property, at their leisure, and to the best advantage, and then, instead (as they themselves would undoubtedly have done, had the situation of the parties been reversed) of seizing upon them, and stripping them of the proceeds of their patrimony, quietly permitted them to sail away, to Holland or anywhere else they might choose to go, unopposed, unobstructed, and unpillaged; rejoicing, no doubt, to be so well rid of so factious and troublesome a crew. They landed in Holland, and with their idolized Pastor, Rev. Mr. Robinson, settled in Leyden.

The Dutch Government, having permitted them to settle within its territory, thenceforth troubled itself but little about them. In fact, the Dutch Government seems wholly to have ignored their very existence. In this it manifested much wisdom. It was, doubtless, fully aware what a factious, troublesome, and pernicious gang they were, and very judiciously left them to their own devices. Here, one would suppose, the Puritans might have rested satisfied. They never pretended, nor have their lying descendants ever pretended for them, that they were persecuted by the Dutch. They were not compelled to contribute to the support of any religion but their own. They had full liberty to worship any Thing or any Being they preferred – God or Baal, or no God at all. They might read or not read the Bible – pray standing, walking, running, riding or lying down – might pray as long and as impiously as suited them. It was perfectly at their own option to act as awkwardly, feel as frigidly, dress as clownishly, sing as discordantly, and snuffle, as abominably, as suited their own wishes and convenience. In short, they could do as they pleased. Few noticed them; still fewer cared for them, or what they did, and none interfered with them.

Thus, it should seem that Holland would have been an elysium, a promised land, to the Puritans, but it did not prove so. Either because they were not persecuted, or more probably, judging by their subsequent history, because they had no one whom they could themselves persecute, their experiment, in Holland, proved a failure. Free from the payment of tithes; exempt from all religious taxation, or vexation of any kind; with full liberty to worship when, where and how they would, and whatever and whomsoever they saw fit, the darling Puritans were discontented and unhappy. Their community, notwithstanding the zealous labors of their beloved Pastor, Rev. Mr. Robinson, dragged out an unsatisfactory and precarious existence for ten years, and then crumbled to pieces. By the advice of the said Pastor, they determined to sail for the New World. On their way they landed, and remained for a short time, in England. Sailing thence for the shores of America, their last act, before bidding a final adieu to their native country, was the inditing and forwarding a letter to the Church of England – that self-same persecuting Church, which had so grievously oppressed them, and against which their descendants have since fulminated so many bitter anathemas, in this letter, which is still extant, there is no rebuke for wrongs received, no complaint of injuries inflicted, no allusion to persecutions suffered. The substance of that letter is an earnest eulogy of the Church of England; an acknowledgment of many and great favors and benefits received from it; a profession of sincere thankfulness for the many obligations conferred upon the writers, and a promise to hold the Church, ever, in affectionate and grateful remembrance! Now, this letter is either true or false, and, whether the one or the other, it is a most unfortunate document for Puritan and Yankee. If true, it proves that all the outcry of Puritan and Yankee about oppression and persecution is wholly and willfully fabricated and untrue; if the letter be false, it proves the Puritans to have been, what all the rest of their history proves them – the most consummate hypocrites, the most abandoned liars, and the most abject and soulless sycophants, the world ever saw.

CHAPTER FOUR

☆　☆　☆　☆

After a cordial and affectionate farewell to the Church of England, the Puritans sailed for the New World, and in due time landed upon the shores of America, and upon that part of the coast which is now embraced within the limits of the State of Massachusetts. Thence, in process of time, and from various causes, they eventually settled, or came into the possession of, the adjoining territory, constituting what is known, at the present day, as the six States of New England.

What an illustrious instance of placability of temper, and forgiving disposition, was manifested by the Puritans, in thus giving to their new country the name of the old one, from which they had fled, suffering martyrs, to escape the terrible ills of oppression and persecution!

Here are the Puritans, on a new soil, free from oppression and persecution; at perfect liberty to enjoy that darling wish of their pure and pious hearts, the blessed privilege of "worshipping God according to the dictates of their own consciences." Surely they will now be contented and happy. In this new world, under the fostering care of their most mild and merciful religion, their strict morality, and their warm affection, not only for each other, but for the whole race of man, a new Eden will arise on the Western Hemisphere; the desert shall blossom like the rose; peace and brotherly love will prevail; and at last, even on this sinful earth, shall be realized and enjoyed that heavenly promise in the song of the Sons of Light, "Peace on earth, and good will to men!" Such a result might have been anticipated by one unacquainted with the past history of the Puritans. Such a result might even, to some extent, have been obtained, had not the Puritans simultaneously proved false to all their lofty and high-sounding pretensions, and true to their more grovelling natures and baser instincts.

Nothing was achieved by them for the improvement of mankind individually, or the melioration of society. Jealousy, bickering, strife, amongst themselves, and treachery, oppression and cruelty to others, are the chief characteristics of that model society established by the Puritans in New England. Upon their first landing, in a bleak climate, in a cold and dreary, season of the year, upon a wild and sterile shore – weak in numbers, weak from long confinement on shipboard, weak from fatigue and disease, and terribly straightened for provisions, they were met by the native lords of the soil, at that time strong enough to have exterminated the weak band of Pilgrims, with a kindness, a courtesy, and a welcome, which would have done honor to an advanced state of civilized or even Christian society. The wild Indian, far superior in the native nobility of his soul, to the fanatical Puritans, pitied their weakness, ministered to their necessities, aided them in their difficulties, and fed them in their hunger. And what was his reward? Treachery the most shameless, and ingratitude the most disgraceful, which blacken the annals of men.

In their first intercourse with the generous, simple-minded, and confiding Aborigines, the Puritans commenced their well-established practices, and manifested their true and inherent character. Then they began that course of deceit, duplicity and chicane, which had rendered them odious in the Old World, and which was to make them infamous in the New. The selfishness, egotism, arrogance and avarice, which had characterized them in Europe, manifested themselves with special or increased strength in America. The lower and baser passions of humanity had been the springs of action with the Puritan; they governed the conduct of the Pilgrim; they have descended unimpaired, and in full force, to their posterity, from generation to generation, and are as surely the characteristic of the Yankee of to-day, as they were of his progenitors in the seventeenth century.

Too weak, in the outset, for conflict with the Indians, the Puritans were content, for the time being, to cheat, to overreach, to defraud them. In this they easily succeeded, and they and their descendants, have made this nefarious success a subject of self-gratulation, and complacent vain-glorying.

With the same spirit of brazen effrontery in which their ancestors claimed "all the religion and all the piety" of their time; in the same unblushing impudence with which the Yankees of the present generation have arrogated to themselves "all the decency and all the morality" of the country, their historians detail the fraudulent transactions of the Puritans, and exult in their successful chicanery.

The historians of the Puritans, and their Yankee descendants, tell us that "the Pilgrims bought the lands of the Indians," and specify the amount paid, as, "a bale of blankets," so many "strings of beads," so many "kegs of rum." Stating thus the vast amount of lands purchased, in tens, and twenties, and fifties of thousands of acres, and the trifling value of the recompense, they plume themselves upon that quality, in their ancestors, which so greatly abounds in themselves; a quality which, in their peculiar parlance, they name "cuteness," but which is known to the rest of the world by the more clear and explicit denomination of fraud.

In these very statements, however, where they openly glory in the shameful dishonesty of their progenitors, which, by a peculiar moral obliquity, appears to be praiseworthy in their eyes – so natural, so constitutional, so innate, is mendacity in them – they do not tell the truth!

What did the Puritans buy from the Indians, and what did the Indians sell? What possible idea had an Indian of the exclusive character of title to land, as title to land was understood in Europe? None whatever. He might have, and did have, an idea of the right to personal property, but none at all of that to real estate. He could, and did sell, or exchange, or give, his skins, his fish, his game, his hunting implements, or his robe of deerskins. These he had caught, or killed, or made. In these he understood there was title, property. While in his possession they were his, exclusively, and no one had any right to them but himself. When he sold or gave them into the possession of another, he fully comprehended that the title, the property in them, passed away from him to the new possessor. He could sell them, for they were his; another could buy them, with his consent, for, being his, he had a right to dispose of them.

But the earth belonged to the Great Spirit, and the

hunting grounds were for the common use of His red children.

True, these hunting grounds were divided out, by imaginary boundaries, amongst different tribes, and one tribe was not allowed to use the hunting grounds of another tribe. This, too, the Indians perfectly understood, but even this gave them no conception of property in land, even by a tribe. The tribes themselves were not stationary, but often changed their hunting grounds. The land was wide, the population small, and a tribe, in removing, took possession of unoccupied hunting grounds. Even the division of the hunting grounds of the country amongst the different tribes seems to have resulted rather from the fact that the normal state of all uncivilized races appears to be that of war, and the desire of all to have some settled and specific territory, in which they might, at times, consider themselves in peace and in safety from hostile efforts, than to have originated in any idea of exclusive possession. In each and every tribe the land was held in common; no one pretended any exclusive title to any portion of it. The habits of the Indians were unsettled and migratory. Their very habitations, light, bark huts, were removable at pleasure. They could be, and often were, removed every few days, and not unfrequently several times the same day.

I repeat it – the Puritans did not buy the title to the land from the Indians, for the Indians never sold it. It is absurd to say that a man has sold what he never dreamed he possessed, and no Indian ever fancied that he had any peculiar and exclusive individual title to any land whatever.

What the Indians sold to the Puritans was the right to occupy and use their hunting grounds in common with themselves. This, and no more, is what they disposed of to the Puritans. Had they, for one moment, supposed that they were then giving into the hands of the Puritans a power by which they would themselves, at a future time, be expelled from the homes of their infancy and the graves of their fathers, they would sooner have shed the last drop of their blood than have consummated the fatal compact. They proved this at a later day, but it was then too late. Their weak and suppliant visitors had become strong. Every ship from the East brought out new bands of adventurers, and soon the foreigners were too strong for the natives.

Then, strong in numbers, and stronger still in the advantage of firearms, the Puritans explained to the Indians the full meaning, and the consequences of what had been done. They had been too discreet, too "cute," as their Yankee successors would say, to be so explicit in the days of their weakness; but now they gave full sway to their passions, full expression to their intentions, in the excellent day of their power. Nothing could exceed the astonishment, the dismay, the indignation of the Indians, when openly told how shamefully they had been overreached. They remonstrated, they entreated, but in vain. Finally, in the desperate resolve of a just indignation, they flew to arms. The struggle was a doubtful and protracted one, but gunpowder finally decided it in favor of the Puritans. The Indians were hunted down like wolves, shot like dogs, scattered, overthrown, destroyed. Brave as they were, there was no hope of success, no opening for escape. They perished by multitudes, by tribes. The Puritans carried on the war against the Indians as they alone, or their descendants, ever carried on war in modern times.

Suffice to say, that they practiced upon the Indians all the outrages, all the cruelties, and the barbarities, which have ever characterized savage and pagan warfare.

It is, probably, not too much to say that the original provocation to the hostilities which so often occurred, was in every case offered by the Puritans. When no other pretence could be found for making war upon the natives, some of the lowest and most degraded of the Puritans (for as, in every abyss of shame, there is still a lower deep – so, even amongst the Puritans, there were some more debased than the others), would visit the homes of the Indians, injure or steal their property, insult the men or outrage the females. The Indian, like all noble natures, never very patient of injury or wrong, suddenly stung to madness, very often washed out the injury in blood. Then the Puritans were in their element. One of the "Elect" had been "murdered," and unsparing war was commenced immediately against the whole tribe of the offender against the majesty of Puritanism. It was pursued with inhuman avidity, and the most remorseless severity.

The tribe, broken and scattered, usually removed towards the West. Thus was tribe after tribe cut to pieces, and driven from their homes, and in this manner did the Puritans become possessed of many and large additions to the hunting grounds at first so very honestly purchased.

Let the brief history of one tribe, marked by no unusual or peculiar features of atrocity, save in its extensive and wholesale character, serve as an example of the Puritan mode of dealing with the Indian race. The Pequods, a tribe of considerable strength and power, stung, no doubt, by insult and outrage, had broken into "rebellion." Rebellion against whom, or what? What right had the Puritans there, or what claim had they on the Pequods to obedience or submission? But this word, "rebellion," was a favorite appellation with the Puritans, as with their Yankee successors, for all those who resisted their encroachments, or opposed their exactions. So the Pequods were in "rebellion." They assembled their forces in a stronghold, and fortified it to the best of their limited ability.

This rude fort was protected by an abattis of felled trees, the branches turned outward, pointed and sharpened. Here the Pequods assembled their whole force, and made their last stand for independence, and existence as a people. Within the fort were collected their families, women and children, and all their little of worldly goods. The Puritan forces, under Captain Church, soon came upon and attacked them. The defence was gallant and desperate. At last firearms again triumphed over the rude weapons of savage war. The Puritans stormed the fort, massacred the defenders, and, setting fire to the wigwams, burned to death the innocent and the guilty (if there were any there guilty of any higher crime than warmly loving, and boldly defending, their country and their personal liberty), the sick and the well, the hale and the wounded, old and young, male and female, man, woman and child, in one general, merciless conflagration.

Some few of the warriors, with the wild energy of desperation, broke through the line of fire, and the still more fatal line of Puritan muskets, and made their escape to the neighboring tribes; but the Pequod tribe was destroyed; it is never heard of more as a nation.

A few prisoners, old men, women and children, taken captive, were sold into slavery.

Thus the Puritans had the credit of inaugurating Indian slavery on this continent, as well as that of being the chief promoters of, and principal actors in, negro slavery and the slave trade. "Honor to whom honor is due!" Let us not deny them their just claim to these two eminent distinctions.

Did an Indian chieftain of marked ability cross the designs of the Puritans, he was disposed of with equal facility, and equal indifference to all the dictates of justice and morality. King Philip, of Mount Hope, was one of these. He was, if I remember aright, the son of one who had loaded them with benefits. But he would not stoop to Puritan sway, and he was doomed. Unable to conquer him in fair battle, or to capture him, they resorted to the blackest treachery and crime to accomplish the still greater crime of his destruction. King Philip had a dear friend, called Sassacus. Sassacus had also another friend, to whom he was much attached. The Puritans caused this friend of Sassacus to be assassinated, and charged King Philip with the crime. By false and lying testimony, they convinced Sassacus of the truth of this villainous slander of King Philip, and stimulated his natural passion for revenge by bribes and threats. Revenge is considered a virtue by an Indian, and Sassacus consented to murder King Philip. By revealing the haunts, habits, and customs of King Philip, and by betraying, with the basest treachery, all the secrets which had been communicated to him in the openness of confiding friendship, after much time had clapsed, and great efforts had been made, the Puritans surrounded King Philip in a swamp, and there he fell, fighting nobly to the last, by a ball from the hand of Sassacus. In a short time Sassacus himself was assassinated, and surely, under the peculiar circumstances, it argues no great want of charity to believe, as I do believe, that he, too, was murdered by the Puritans. The wife of King Philip, and his infant son, were captured by his Puritan enemies, and both – the one a prince, and the other the daughter and mother of a prince, and the wife, or rather the widow, of a king were promptly sold, by these mild, charitable, forgiving, Christian Puritans, into life-long slavery in the West Indies.

The fate of the remnant, the small fragment, of the Indian tribes who escaped death on the battlefield, and slavery, and who, instead of fleeing to the wilderness of the West, remained within the limits of Puritandom, was scarcely less melancholy, and far less reputable. Without home, tribe, or occupation, they wandered about in listless apathy, and soon became worthless vagabonds. By associating with the white, they lost all the virtues of the red man, and soon acquired, in great perfection, all the vices, of the Puritan – all save one. In lying they could never even approach their great exemplars. The Puritans supplied them freely with rum, and the fire-water soon completed their utter degradation.

They became the victims of new and unknown diseases, contracted by their association with the Puritans, but never seen or heard of by their own people.

They wasted away, and finally perished from the earth. Not two centuries had elapsed from the landing of the Pilgrims, and the Indian race was extinct in New England. They were dead, in slavery, or gone far towards the setting sun, so apt an emblem of the fate of their race.

The Puritans could, no doubt, easily justify themselves for all these enormities, by a few texts from the Old Testament; such, for example, as, "And Asael arose and executed judgment;" "Slay the heathen with the edge of the sword;" or, "Hew Agag in pieces before the Lord;" and their worthy successors can even find cause of laudation in such devilish deeds; but history and posterity, will, and have, reversed this judgment, and will yet hold the character and conduct of the Puritans up to a sterner test, and before a more equitable and more august audience than that of their own pliant conscience, or that of their complaisant descendants.

CHAPTER FIVE

☆　☆　☆　☆

While such, and so ineffably infamous, had been the conduct of the Puritans toward the Indians, let us examine what was its character to each other, and towards the rest of their own race. Even at the very outset of their career, while scheming, intriguing, and overreaching the Indians for the possession of the soil, they were quarreling and striving fiercely amongst themselves for the attainment of political power, and religious domination.

No sooner had these poor, honest, charitable and philanthropic exiles – these virtuous refugees from oppression and persecution – these sturdy sticklers for entire political and religious freedom and equality – found the time and the place where they held the supremacy, than they, at once, proceeded to enact laws of terrible severity against all who presumed to differ with them in creed or in practice.

The Puritans attempted, and that most faithfully, to establish a government upon the purest theocratic regulations, with themselves as the high priests and the rulers.

Everyone was required to conform his belief to the

requirements of the Puritan creed, and to square his conduct by the Puritan code of morals and of manners. Every individual was compelled, by their laws, to a prompt and regular attendance at their places of worship. Absence from the meeting house, and the usual ministrations there, was readily construed into heresy, the punishment for which offence was most prompt and severe, embracing, as it did, public reprimand and open rebuke, fine, imprisonment, the pillory and the stocks, with a very intelligible indication of an ultimate resort, in case of persistent contumacy, to the stake or the gibbet. Under the pressure of arguments so conclusive, and so potent, the attendance of the Puritan societies upon the ministrations of their "pastors," in the "Sanctuary," and on the "Sabbath day" especially, was most satisfactory and exemplary.

All attended upon these religious ministrations, for if the love of God did not draw, the fear of man drove them there. Of the character of those ministrations, it is sufficient to say that they consisted chiefly of long prayers, and longer sermons. The nature of these sermons may, in some measure be estimated from the fact that, the Bible having been excluded from their pulpits, as too much like the Church, the preacher selected, at his pleasure, some isolated passage of Scripture, and made this text the – at least professed – subject and foundation of his long discourse. This text he explained, enlarged upon, twisted or perverted, according to his own fancy, his passions, his prejudices, or his general fanaticism; generally improving the occasion by a fulsome laudation of his own creed and his own particular sect, or his own special congregation, and a fierce and bitter denunciation of all the world besides, and anathematizing them with all the ills and all the woes his memory could retain, or his imagination conjure up, both here and hereafter, for time and for eternity. In civil affairs Puritan rule was no less exacting or severe. All heretics, by which term they modestly designated all the world outside the pale of their own bigoted sect, were wholly excluded from "all offices of honor, profit or trust." Nay, more, the very employment of such unhallowed persons, even in the most menial capacity, as a day laborer, as a servant, as a household drudge, was fiercely denounced, and strictly forbidden. In politics and in religion, the Puritan must needs be supreme. The earth was the Lord's – the Puritans, the Elect, the Saints, were the children of the Lord and, of course, entitled to the possession and sovereignty of the earth. No others had any rights whatever, personal, political or religious. Indeed, how was it possible, in the nature of things, that they should have any right at all, even the right of existence? Were they not, in very truth, the children of Belial? Having speedily established matters on this comfortable and satisfactory footing, the Puritans soon took another step. They were then, as now, a nation of progress. Having then, as in more recent times, secured all, and more than all, which was their own, they began to look about them to see what they could steal or rob from others.

In this quest their peculiar character, and the skill acquired from long and successful practice in chicane, soon insured them signal success. Having robbed the Indians of their land, they began to rob each other. Soon they robbed Roger Williams and his followers of their possessions, and, by persecution, drove them into exile. Delighted with their success, and intoxicated with the luxurious flavor of this taste of persecution, they turned their attention to the Quakers. The mild and peaceable lives of this quiet sect, their meek, subdued, and orderly manners, their strict morality, and their undoubted integrity, were no recommendation, in the eyes of the saintly Puritans, and afforded them no protection. They were expelled, banished, driven out from the society of the meek, mild, charitable and compassionate Puritans, as though they had been attainted and convicted felons. Nay, more – these immaculate Saints, these Christians par excellence, these Chosen and Elect, who had but a short time ago been so loud, so vociferous, and so vehement, in their outcries against persecution – proceeded, forthwith, to the enactment of certain wise, salutary, humane, and philanthropic laws in behalf of the Quakers. By these laws, it was decreed that in case of the return of a banished Quaker, he should be branded with the letter "H," as a heretic; if he attempted to preach or promulgate his religious opinions, that he should have his tongue bored through with a red hot iron; and finally, that for the second offence, he should be hanged! This, be it distinctly understood, was to be done solely on account of his religious creed, for neither the false-hearted Puritans nor his lying descendants, the Yankees, have ever alleged any other crime against them. These brutal, and worse than savage laws were enacted, and in some cases, wherever opportunity offered, enforced, by those zealous advocates, those devoted apostles of, and those self-sacrificing exiles and martyrs to, the doctrine and principle of "perfect independence in religion, and entire freedom of conscience"! Oh! shame, where is thy blush? The Puritans, not content to rule in all civil and religious matters, soon proceeded to interfere with, and legislate for, the direction of private conduct and domestic affairs. Like their Yankee descendants, they were all meddlers and busy-bodies.

The "Saybrook Platform," the old "Blue Laws of

Connecticut," remain to this day, a monument of the bigotry, folly and intolerance of the Puritan, and an object of scorn, of ridicule and contempt, to all the world. It is enough to say of them, that they proscribed all the natural affections, and forbade every manifestation of them, however harmless and innocent. As an example, "a man was fined for kissing his wife, on his return from a long and dangerous sea voyage," and narrowly escaped the whipping-post – the latter affair being in a most especial manner a Puritan "institution." All traveling on the "Sabbath" was strictly prohibited, and the prohibition as strictly enforced. No matter how urgent the necessity, or how terrible the reason for traveling, on the "Sabbath" it must cease. Though the parent were flying to the sick or dying bed of the child, or the husband to that of the wife, if a "Sabbath " intervened ere the goal was reached, the afflicted traveler and the suffering patient were separated by a chasm as impassable as the gulf which yawned between Abraham and Dives. Even in sight of the very house containing the sick, or the dying, the agonized traveler could not move a step until "sundown" had indicated the close of the Puritan "Sabbath," though, in the meantime, the sick one, whether father or mother, son or daughter, brother or sister, husband or wife, breathed existence away, and passed, unseeing, and unseen by the loved one, though so near, through the shadow of the dark valley.

At a loss how further to annoy and harass humanity, the Puritans happily fell upon the notable device of Witchcraft. This afforded a glorious field for the display of Puritan intolerance, bigotry, malignity and cruelty, and for a considerable time they flourished and luxuriated in it without stint or limit.

If I do not err, the Puritans may justly claim all the

credit of having been the first to commit murder, in Europe, on the plea of witchcraft; it is certain they inaugurated it on this continent, where they were the first, and only persons, who ever burned witches, as they were the last in this country, as well as the last in Christendom, to discontinue the atrocity. Lest some few of my readers may not fully remember, or comprehend, what is meant by witchcraft, in the Puritan sense of the word, I shall, in as brief terms as possible, endeavor to explain it, as it appeared in New England. There is usually, in almost every community, one or more poor, innocent, harmless, but helpless old woman, who, having survived all of her cotemporaries, is unconnected with any immediate relatives, and usually lives alone. Now, in Puritan times, such old women, so situated, were not uncommon. Some weak and sickly child from the peevishness of illness, from a naturally malicious disposition, or prompted by older persons, would have, or pretend to have, fits, spasms, convulsions, and being interrogated, would name one of these unfortunate old women, and charge her with being the cause of this suffering, and with having bewitched him. The poor old woman was instantly arrested. Removed from her melancholy home, where, in all probability, she was passing away the waning hours of her harmless and helpless life in sorrowful meditation upon the evanescent character of all human happiness, or speculations on the mysteries of that unknown world to which she must soon depart. She was hurried before her accusers, and at the same time her judges. The pious conclave – the Pastor and the Elders – assembled rapidly as the vultures at the scent of blood, gravely inform her that she is accused of witchcraft. Of course, she promptly denies the charge. But this is all she can do. From the absurdity of the charge, and the intangibility of evidence in such a case, the charge can neither be proved nor disproved. And here, with her denial, one would suppose the matter would end by the dismissal of the poor creature, in peace, to her home. Nothing of the kind. All honor to the Puritans! They had discovered an infallible method of detecting a witch. Where reason, logic, and common sense wholly failed, they met with magnificent success. By a method, the wisdom and originality of which is all their own, and for whose mildness, gentleness and humanity, they may justly claim all the credit and all the glory, they were enabled to put the question of witchcraft beyond all doubt or cavil. This brilliant discovery was practiced in the following manner:

They tied the old woman, accused of witchcraft, hand and foot, and plunged her headlong into deep water! If she sank, she was innocent – but in that case she was drowned; if she swam, she was guilty – and thereupon she was burned! In either case, whether innocent or guilty, she was sure to perish. To be accused of witchcraft was, to the old and helpless, death; and this wanton wasting of human life was occasioned by the malice of a vindictive brat, the only notice of whose accusation should have been a sound flogging, and the ignorance, bigotry and superstitious cruelty of Pastors and Elders, to whom justice would have awarded the halter. This madness made its first appearance in Salem, in the State of Massachusetts – a State which has been the hotbed, from that day till now, of every grovelling superstition, and every fanatical creed, and every bigoted sect, which have vexed and disgraced humanity. This madness, however, was not confined to Salem, nor even to Massachusetts. The taste of the Puritan for persecution was too strong, his enjoyment of human suffering, and the shedding of human blood, too keen, for witchcraft to be confined to such narrow limits. It spread like wild-fire over all the domain of the Puritans. While only the poor and the lowly suffered, its progress was onward, and its desolating career unopposed. Pastors and Elders swam with the tide. Even Cotton Mather, the Magnus Apollo of the Yankees, of whose learning, eloquence and piety they so loudly boast, was one of the witch-hunters and witch-burners. At last those gifted children who pointed out the witches, grown bolder by impunity, designated some of the Elders and Pastors as the wicked witches, or wizards, who tormented them. This was going too for, and the step proved fatal to witchcraft. The sacred caste had been attacked, and it rallied, *en masse*, for the destruction of the enemy. Witchcraft was declared, by the Pastors, to be absurd, and the stories of the afflicted children incredible. The children were soundly beaten, their abettors punished, and witchcraft disappeared from the world. To New England, however, belongs the distinguished honor of having afforded witchcraft its last resting place on earth. There it spread more rapidly, ravaged more extensively, and continued longer and more persistently, than in any other land. There it held its last grand carnival of grief and suffering, of agony and blood.

The ultimate existence, the last struggle, the final triumph, of witchcraft, were all reserved to grace, in an appropriate manner, with their waning glories, the favored land of the Puritan.

I have now finished my sketch of the character and history of the progenitors of our present Abolition enemies, under the several names of Independents, Puritans and Pilgrims. I have shown what they have done, by the records of the past, by which we may fairly judge what they will do in the future, should their power ever suffice to carry out their intentions. I have little further to say of them, until the time of the American Revolution, when, and subsequent to which, the conduct and character of their descendants – whom, merging all other names, I shall hereafter designate solely as Yankee Abolitionists – will require, and shall receive, my special attention.

Of the Puritans, from the days of witchcraft to the Revolution, it will be sufficient to say that their conduct, under all circumstances, was characteristic and consistent, and just was, judging from their previous career, what we should naturally look for in such a people. Their actions, in every relation in life, both amongst themselves and in their intercourse with others, continued, always marked by the same ignoble cunning, the same disingenuousness, the same intense selfishness, and the same total disregard of the rights of others, which have been the marked characteristic of the Puritan race in all their preceding history.

CHAPTER SIX

☆ ☆ ☆ ☆

We have now traced the history and the conduct of the ancestors of our Abolition enemies down to the era of the Revolution. The descendants of these execrable progenitors had at that period become known, and are still known, all over the world by the name of Yankees – a name now become synonymous with trickster and cheat, and infamous wherever known, under the wide canopy of heaven. They caused the outbreak of the American Revolution, as their sires had that of England. In precipitating this revolution they, as their forefathers had done, made loud professions of pure principle, and lofty, patriotic feelings. But we know them better now, and distrust their fair pretensions. We have learned, by experience, that whenever the Yankees are loudest in their professions of disinterested and pure motives, then we must look most closely for actions springing from, and controlled by, the grossest cupidity and selfishness. They have taught us that their most lofty professions of pure intentions, and magnanimous principles, are the invariable precursors of some base action; that when they announce their conduct as the result of upright and honorable impulses, we are to suspect them strongly of selfish motives and sinister intentions. In this manner, and in this manner only, can we judge them correctly, and do ourselves justice.

The Yankees brought on the war by their resistance to the payment of a tax on stamped paper, and afterwards upon tea. They professed that the tax was as nothing in their eyes, but it was the "principle!" "Taxation," said they, "without representation, is tyranny," and we are resolved to resist that tyranny. The profession was specious, and the principle stated in the maxim true enough. Still I, for one, cannot give full credence to this Yankee profession. Judging by the past history of their fathers, and the subsequent history of themselves, I am compelled to doubt them, and to receive their statement *cum grano salis*. Knowing the unbounded adoration then, and ever since, paid by them to the "Almighty Dollar," the depth of their devotion to and their sedulous worship at the shrine of Mammon, I am compelled to suspect the purity of their very plausible professions, and to suspect that interest had more influence upon their conduct than principle; in a word, I am forced to the conclusion that their determined resistance was rather the result of an unwillingness to loosen their purse-strings than an ardent attachment to liberty, and an unselfish devotion to the cause of human rights and political independence. This conclusion is forced upon me the more irresistibly, because their pecuniary interests, at the time, were involved in the question of political freedom, and that the only mode left for them, by which to save their money, was to advocate and support the cause of liberty; and still further than this, in no instance, either before or since, which I can recollect, have the Yankees ever manifested any very warm or zealous interest in the cause of liberty, unless that cause contributed, in some manner, to their own emolument and advantage.

But the Yankees succeeded in their intentions. Boston Harbor was blockaded. The Southern colonies accepted the plausible professions of the Yankees as the true expression of their sentiments. At all events, the doctrine of the Yankees, as contained in the maxim of Otis, already quoted, was true; it met the approbation of the Southerners; they sympathised with the Yankees in their privations and sufferings, embraced their party, made common cause with them against Great Britain, joined freely in the struggle, and after an eight years' war, succeeded in winning independence for the Yankees, and, as they supposed, for themselves. The Yankees, true to their instincts, and the principles imparted by sire to son for ten generations, have repaid them with characteristic ingratitude! Here I must beg leave to remark that, by the word Yankee, I do not confine myself to the inhabitants of the New England States, for I include all who emigrated to the Abolition States, and the natives of all places where their principles have extended and their doctrines and practices been adopted. Nor do I include in the term, as I use it, as one of shame and reproach, those who, although born in New England, are free from the vices and fanaticism of the land of their birth. There have been many good and worthy men born even in New England, else had she, long since, met the fate of Sodom and Gomorrah! Many of these noble men are fighting gallantly, in our ranks, for Southern independence; of course I do not mean these. By Yankee I mean a bigot, a fanatic, and an Abolitionist, be he born where he may, and I call him Yankee, in the opprobrious sense of the word, because Yankeeland was the hotbed from which the vile fanaticism sprang, and the greater part of its children are the propagandists of the fanatical doctrine. In my usage of the term, a man of Southern feeling, actuated by Southern principles, is a Southerner, and an Abolitionist is a Yankee – be they born where they may.

In this connection, permit me to say a few words upon Abolition and the slave trade. Thirty years ago, in a public address made in a Northern college, in the early history of Abolitionism, I stated "that the Abolitionists were the legitimate, or at least lineal, descendants of those who had stolen the negroes from Africa, and sold them to our ancestors in the South, and that they, these descendants, would, if they ever had the opportunity, steal them anew and sell them over again." The history of the present war has amply verified my assertion.

The English nation, which has since, like the Yankees, run mad on the subject of slavery, was the first to fasten it upon the Southern colonies by force, despite their opposition, entreaties and remonstrances.

At first the English were the great purveyors of slaves for the Southern colonies, but they were soon rivalled and outstripped, in this infamous contest for gold, by the Yankees. Hundreds of Yankee ships, with entire Yankee crews, sailed for the coast of Africa, and, on their return, brought back hundreds of thousands of the Africans they had bought, or stolen, to the planters of the South. Wilberforce and his fanatical followers, in their terrible descriptions of the horrors of "the middle passage," are silent as to the share the English had in these atrocities. The Yankee sentimentalists, who have gloried in their descriptions of the awful nature of this "middle passage," and have painted it in the most direful colors, alike ignore the share taken by their ancestors.

They carefully avoid the truth, as usual. One would suppose, in reading their wild ravings, that the slave trade had been carried on by Southerners alone, and that the hands of their progenitors were, in this matter, "clean every whit." They fraudulently omit to state, what is the real truth, that, so far as the colonies were concerned, the slave trade was carried on by Yankee capital, by Yankee sailors and by Yankee bottoms, alone. They studiously refrain from admitting another fact, equally true and incontrovertible, which is, that all the "horrors of the middle passage," which so afflict their delicate sensibilities, arose from the grasping avarice and relentless cruelty of their Yankee forefathers. The Yankee slave traders, with characteristic avarice and inhumanity, allowed to the poor negroes subjected to their control the very narrowest amount of space which could contain the human frame, and the very least modicum of air, water, and food, which could support human life, and this even when crossing "the Line!" Thence, and thence alone, arose all the unnecessary sufferings, all the revolting "horrors of the middle passage." *Fiat justicia!*

When, after the acknowledgment of the independence of the United States, Congress passed an act for the suppression of the slave trade, the Yankees, still deeply interested in the traffic, by their entreaties and their influence succeeded in suspending its operation for some ten years – from 1798 to 1808. So much for Yankee history in connection with the slave trade; and now, having placed them right upon the record, I must return to the beginning of the national history of the United States, from which I have been led away by this digression relative to slavery, and examine into the conduct and character of the Yankees, from that period to the disruption of the old Union, and in fact, up to the present time. We shall find, in this examination, much food for reflection, and many items of information and instruction, which, if well considered and properly improved, may be of great service to us in the future, by pointing out to us the hidden dangers, the shoals, and the quicksands of the past. By properly heeding these beacons of experience, our new organization may, haply, escape the dangers and difficulties which have rent the old.

The Yankees, having succeeded in suspending, or postponing, the operation of the law for the suppression of the slave trade plunged into that traffic with renewed energy, and redoubled diligence. The ocean "was whitened by the canvass of Yankee ships, bearing their cargoes, by thousands and hundreds of thousands, to the markets of the Southern States. This continued as long as they could find purchasers; until, in fact, to use a mercantile expression, they had "glutted" the slave market. Then, after having pocketed the last dollar they could hope to make off this very honest and honorable manner, they sold their ships and other appliances for carrying on the slave trade, or diverted them into other channels, joined, open-mouthed, in the loud clamor against the slave trade, commenced their pious enterprise of Abolition, and proclaimed, at least by impudent assumption, their zealous philanthropy, and earnest affection for the whole African race!

How consistent with this proceeding has been the course of their successors!

How often have we seen the Yankee, fresh from his home of bigotry, superstition and intolerance, in the North, settle down among us, and eventually become the owner of negro property? How often have we seen him

come into the possession of negroes, either through syco-
phancy, fawning and flattery, by marriage, or through cunning, tergiversation, and overreaching by purchase? And
what is the result? As a general rule, they make the very
worst masters in the whole South; exact more labor, feed
and clothe their slaves worse, and punish them more fre-
quently, and far more severely, than any Southern slaveholder. Some of them remain here permanently, and become good masters and worthy citizens, but many more of
them, after securing a fortune, return to the more congenial atmosphere of New England, which is so admirably
suited in its false pretensions, venality and hypocrisy, to
their own degraded natures. They remain amongst us long
enough to know the groundless nature of their former
ideas of slavery, and the utter and shameless falsehood of
the thousand and one slanderous and malicious Yankee
tales of slavery and slaveholders; and no sooner are they
once more settled in Yankeedom, than their natural falsehood and bigotry seem to spring into renewed, and more
active existence, as if invigorated and strengthened by
their long suppression. They become, at once, red hot,
rampant, open-mouthed Abolitionists. All the vile and
slanderous tales against Southerners and the South, which
they once believed through ignorance, and repeated from
bigotry, they now, knowing them to be entirely untrue,
endorse through self-interest and fanaticism, and propagate from malice. They tell all, and more than all, that they
have seen and heard, or even imagined against the South,
but there is one thing they are especially careful not to tell;
that is, how they, themselves, cleared their skirts of the
"crying sin" of slaveholding! They studiously avoid this
subject, and it is wise in them to do so, for the truth would
be little to their credit, and a falsehood would be too easily

detected and exposed. I do not greatly censure them for their silence. A lie, though so easy and so natural to them, would not answer their purpose; and the truth, besides being disgraceful, is so strange to, and uncongenial with, Yankee nature, that to tell it, on this or any other occasion, would, doubtlessly, have required a laborious and painful effort! I will tell the truth for them, sparing them the exertion, though I cannot shield them from the mortification.

Wholly unlike, in this as in everything else, the Southern slave-holder, who carefully nurtures, feeds, and clothes his negroes, nurses them in sickness, and decently buries them after death, the Yankee master, when he has resolved to return to his New England paradise, immediately sells all his slaves, to the last one, to the highest bidder, and utterly indifferent who the new owner may be, or what kind of a master he may make. The conscientious Yankee, having thus relieved himself from the taint of slaveholding, pockets the money, departs for his congenial home, and never troubles his thoughts again with his deserted slaves, any more than if they were of the beasts which perish, or senseless stocks and stones! Who ever heard of a Yankee slaveholder emancipating his negroes? To use his own characteristic language, this "would not pay." Now, Yankees never do anything which they think will not pay; this, in their opinion and language, would manifest, on their part, a very discreditable want of their usual "cuteness." I doubt if there be a single well authenticated instance of a Yankee slaveholder liberating his negroes, under any circumstances whatever.

Many Southern slaveholders have not only emancipated their negroes, but paid their passage to Liberia, and furnished them with a liberal outfit of clothing, provisions, and working implements, sufficient to support them for the first year, and enable them to enter fairly and easily upon a new life in their new home. The wisdom of this action on the part of these Southern slave-holders may be doubted, but the purity of their motives, and the kindness and thoughtfulness of their conduct, are certainly, according to Yankee ethics at least, beyond all question. Does any one of my readers remember, or has he ever heard of, a Yankee slaveholder who has adopted the same course towards *his* negroes? For my own part, I must confess I do not know of one single instance of the kind.

The returned Yankee, in the congenial atmosphere and society of his Northern home, becomes immediately a fiery Abolitionist. His fanaticism and intolerance having been so long repressed in the South, he is like a new convert, and the zeal of his proselyting is unlimited. Now he luxuriates in shameless slanders of the manners, customs, morals, and people of the South; now he denounces them in unmeasured and unsparing terms. Having lived in the South, he is accepted as an authority on all Southern questions by his Yankee comrades. During his residence in the South he may have heard of some instances of oppression or cruelty inflicted upon a slave. This may or may not be true, for there are some unkind, and occasionally, though rarely, a cruel master, even amongst the Southerners. This I do not wish to deny, for, unlike the Yankees, we of the South have never claimed the right "to throw the first stone" at anyone, on the ground that we were "ourselves without sin."

This instance of oppression or cruelty, exceptional and isolated as he knows it to be, if it be true at all, the returned Yankee reproduces to his Northern audience, garbled, misstated, falsely colored, and wilfully exaggerated. Spiced and seasoned to suit the morbid taste of Abolition fanaticism, he represents it as the usual treatment of slaves by their masters, and a fair example of the character of slavery in the whole South! His fanatical audiences believe, or profess to believe him, and his story is inserted into the Abolition papers, scattered broadcast through the country, and made the ground of new slander, and denunciation of the South. Having catered to the base appetites and vile natures of the Abolition pack, the returned Yankee is applauded, caressed and feted. He becomes a great man in his little circle, and receives such honor as they can confer upon him. Virtuous leader! amiable followers! worthy associates! Long may he enjoy the dignified position he has so creditably attained, and long may his pious followers be enlightened by his lofty intelligence, and purified by the bright example of his stainless morality! Had he told them the truth, they would not have believed him, or had they believed him, so unwelcome and unpalatable would the truth have been to them, they would have hissed, hooted, and probably mobbed him. In telling them a base falsehood, he has secured their good will. The story he has related accords with their preconceived opinions, confirms their prejudices, and gratifies their animosity to the South; and so he is welcomed and honored, so far as they can confer honor, by a false-hearted and treacherous generation, which seems, in the just retribution of an avenging Providence, to have been "given over," in their vices, their follies and their impiety, "to believe a delusion and a lie."

CHAPTER SEVEN

☆ ☆ ☆ ☆

The mode of proceeding, and the means used, by the Yankees, in delaying for ten years the enforcement of the law for the suppression of the slave trade, now deserve a little consideration. By the same proceedings and the same means, they have succeeded in effecting all their subsequent sectional, unjust, class legislation, through which they have enriched themselves from the plunder and spoils of the South, gained under color of law. The proceedings were the genuine, natural result of the Yankee character, and may be summed up in the words, electioneering, deception, misrepresentation, bribery and fraud.

The principal means consisted in their unequal and unjust preponderance, through their representatives, in the Senate of the United States. The system of representation adopted by our Government, in the House of Representatives, gave one representative, in that House, for so many thousands of population. This was fair and just, for it was the same in the whole country, and operated equally and equitably in every State. But in the Senate of the United States, every State was represented by two delegates, and this was neither fair nor just. By the operation of this law of representation, States of the smallest extent and most limited population, had as many Senators as States the largest in territory and greatest in numbers. Rhode Island had as many Senators as Virginia, Delaware as Carolina. By the operation of this very unequal mode of representation it has, not unfrequently, occurred, that a State whose population gave it but one representative in the House of Representatives, while the rule gave it two members in the Senate. In the earlier years of our Government, the five Yankee States held ten of the twenty-six seats in the Senate, or nearly half of them. By means of this solid phalanx, always voting together on all sectional questions, aided by intrigue, barter, and corruption by the Yankees amongst the other Senators, and the Representatives. Generally, they succeeded in staying the operation of the law for the suppression of the slave trade, and in passing almost any act they wished, for their own aggrandizement or the advancement of their pecuniary interest. The Yankees, opposed to all monopolies against them, but the greatest monopolists the world ever has seen yet, when the monopoly was for their benefit, succeeded, from the commencement of United States history until the dissolution of the Union, by the means above indicated, in securing to themselves a very large share of all the power, patronage and benefits of the Government. Engaged in whaling, and other fisheries, they desired the aid of the Government money, and they obtained it in the form of "Bounty." They wished to extend their internal trade, and by the aid of "internal improvements," most unjustly and unequally distributed, aside from their unconstitutionality, they succeeded in this also. They succeeded in monopolizing the whole coasting trade, by the passage of navigation acts.

Embarked most extensively in manufactures, they managed to destroy competition by the enactment of high tariffs, which, while enriching them, were an unjust and onerous tax upon the South. By the operation of the Patent Laws, and the construction they put upon them, they monopolized the benefit of the genius, the labor and the ingenuity of all nations.

By refusing the enactment of a law of "International Copyright," they reserved to themselves the power of plundering the literary treasure of the world. In their efforts to plunder the U.S. Treasury on a grand scale, or to overreach the South, or swindle other countries magnificently, the Yankees generally resorted to the machinery of Congressional legislation, and almost invariably with abundant success. It is, I believe, no exaggeration to say that the Yankees, with a population less than a fourth, and a territory not more than a twentieth of the old United States, managed, for half a century, to appropriate to their own benefit three-fourths of the public money expended for the improvement of commerce and the defence of the country; as may yet be seen in the internal improvements, harbor improvements, light-houses and fortifications, from which the North alone has derived benefit and protection. While such was the nature of the transactions between the Yankees and the South in a National capacity, let us inquire what was the character of their dealings with us as individuals, and in private relations.

Scarcely had the thunders of war ceased – scarcely had the Southerners enjoyed a brief respite from the toils, the sacrifices, and the sufferings, incident to repelling a foreign invasion – when the whole South was inundated by a flood of Yankee peddlers.

If there be any one occupation in the pursuit of

money more thoroughly characterized by, and more entirely the embodiment of, lying, swindling, chicanery and fraud, than any other, it is that of peddling; and of all peddlers, the Yankees have abundantly proved themselves the most eminently endowed with all the debasing qualities, and all the infamous practices characteristic of this vile and dirty trade. The Yankees, with their worthless merchandise, mounted every hill and traversed every valley in the South. Soon the whole country was filled with the worthless trash which, by unscrupulous and barefaced lying, they had palmed off upon a people thoroughly honest, and because honest, confiding. In city and town, in village and hamlet, on plantation and in cabin, on every hand, and in every house, were to be seen these evidences of Yankee craft, and testimonies of the success of Yankee fraud. Clocks that would keep no time; tin-ware that would hold no water; broadcloths, cassimeres and domestic goods, which would do no service; ginghams and calicoes whose colors would stand no washing – all of Yankee manufacture, and all worthless, were scattered broadcast through the land. The name of Yankee peddler became, at once, and has never ceased to be, a term of opprobrium, of scorn, and of contempt. The Yankee peddler's cart was regarded with as much abhorrence and loathing, and in some measure of dread, as was the "dead cart" in Europe, during the ravages and horrors of the Plague.

In addition to the curse of Yankee peddlers, Yankee schoolmasters, in swarms, soon flooded the fair regions of the South, bringing with them their nasal twang, their false morality, their proscriptive religion, and their fanatical opinions.

Long and grievously was the South afflicted by these, and various other portions of the Yankee race. Useless, disliked, worthless like the thistle, like the thistle they were ineradicable. Scorned, despised, insulted, and justly trampled on by an outraged and insulted people, the Yankee, true to his training and his instincts, bore all, suffered all, endured all, with fawning and crouching humility. In the pursuit of his idol, the "Almighty Dollar," no humiliations were too degrading, no sacrifices of self-respect, or of the regard of others, too great, so that he, at last, succeeded in winning the deity of his worship – Mammon! Meantime, his Yankee brethren at home were equally busy, in various ways, in the same eager and unscrupulous pursuit of gold. The press groaned beneath the burden imposed by their unflagging efforts; books, pamphlets, magazines, newspapers, in countless thousands, flooded the South. On all subjects, by all authors, and written in all styles, with the sole end of making money in view, nothing was too good, or too bad for them to print, so that it would only sell. The same editors prepared, and the same presses issued, the Bible and the Koran – the sermons of Cotton Mather and the writings of Thomas Paine – the ethics of Paley and the infidelity of Voltaire – pious psalms and profane songs – moral essays and licentious romances – all in one general, indiscriminate and unregarded medley of confusion.

If the great end of money-making was attained, what, to the Yankee, mattered the means? But this is only one phase of Yankee character – only, one face of this more than Janus-visaged people. These several occupations, vile and infamous as they were, although steeped in iniquity, in fraud, and in immorality were still far too innocent to engross the energies or circumscribe the efforts of the pious and virtuous Yankee race. In every country in which the Yankees or their progenitors have, for the sins of mankind, been planted, they have sprung, at once, into a malevolent and noxious existence, more instinct with evil and potent for destruction than the armed fruit of the fabled dragon's teeth of Cadmus. They are, ever have been, and, so long as they are suffered to exist, they ever will be the Arabs of the moral and religious world. "Their hand is against every man's, and every man's hand is against theirs" – or at least, every man's should be.

Of such a race, so impatient of good, so eager for evil to others, it was not to be expected that they should long remain quiet, and contented with the comparatively innocent amusement of deceiving, defrauding, and slandering the Southern people. True to their character and their history, they soon manifested their impatience with occupations which, though in some measure gratifying; to their ignoble natures, still restricted their peculiar genius for evil within such narrow bounds. They had tasted the luxury of blood, and had not forgotten its pleasant flavor. They had enjoyed the delights of persecuting, and were anxious to renew the enjoyment. True and lineal descendants, both in blood and creed, from the assassins of Archbishop Sharpe, the murderers of Dr. Servetus and the burners of witches, they grieved over the pleasures and the glories of the "good old times," and were eager to reproduce them once more. But how could this be brought about? The question was not a difficult one. Though the Yankees, in morals, in religion, and in feeling, had remained stationary for over two centuries, the world had not. It was not easy to renew, in the nineteenth century, the atrocities which had disgraced the sixteenth and the seventeenth. Persecution, for opinion's sake, was no longer the creed or the practice of Christendom. Men had come, generally, to the conclusion that the boot and the thumb-screw, the halter and the faggot, and other ingenious and praiseworthy Calvinistic and Puritan devices, were not the most conclusive of arguments. Hanging, burning, racking and quartering heretics, would no longer be tolerated. But Yankee zeal, cruelty and fanaticism, were not to be baulked of their ends by such obstacles. True, the body had escaped their power. The perversity of man, the "total depravity" of human nature in the nineteenth century, would no longer permit these holy Yankee propagandists to light the fires of physical persecution, or torture the bodies of unbelievers. Still they had, happily, a last resource. The higher, the nobler, the spiritual part of man, was not yet wholly beyond the reach of their power and their vengeance. The offending bodies were beyond the reach even of Yankee intolerance and Yankee ingenuity, but what a glorious, what a delightful discovery! They could yet break the mind upon the wheel of public opinion – they could still "crucify the soul!"

Delighted with this brilliant discovery, the Yankees proceeded to put it into beneficent operation.

They made their first essay upon the Masonic fraternity. Anti-Masonry sprung up suddenly in New England and soon became mad and rampant.

Here I must hasten to pay a just tribute to New England. This is the genial home of Puritan history, and the native land of Yankee fanaticism. Here we find the very locality in which the fable of Heathen Mythology was reduced to fact. Here was opened the true box of Pandora, filled with all the ills, the afflictions, and the misfortunes of the human family; and from New England they have flown abroad to harass and destroy the human race. The Yankees having opened the box, incited by that impudent inquisitiveness and impertinent curiosity for which they have a world-wide renown, continued to hold it open, while making a thorough investigation of its mysteries, until even Hope escaped and fled far away. From New England have sprung more sects in religion, factions in politics, and parties in social life, than from all the world besides. Either of entire native growth, or instantly naturalized in the congenial atmosphere of Yankeedom, New England has produced more superstitions, fanaticisms and follies, than all the rest of Christendom. She is the very land and native soil of all absurdities whose names terminate in "ism." For illustration I will mention a few, and only a few of them, for truly their name is legion. In Yankeedom, in that same New England, we find Witchcraft, Mormonism, Matthiasism, Spiritualism, Millerism, Fourierism, Mesmerism, and Abolitionism – and, I greatly fear, no little Atheism. Here sprang up table-turnings, spirit-rappings, spirit communications, Unitarianism, Universalism, Deism; here arose model artists, and free love societies; here began animal magnetism and Biology. Here we may find Hicksites, Millerites, Truerites, Tompkinsites, and any other kind of "ites." Here we may see Universalians, Unitarians, Trinitarians, Arians – any kind of "arians," even barbarians; and here we may meet with Shakers and Tunkers. This list contains but a tithe, a mere fraction, of the names of the multitude of sects and factions with which Yankeedom is rife.

      This sketch, brief as it is, of the nature and extent of the various and discordant elements into which Yankee society is divided, is a necessary preliminary to the examination of the folly and presumptuous claims, to pre-eminence over others, of the Yankee race. With a modest assurance, characteristic of the Yankees, and wholly unrivalled by any other people, they claim a decided superiority over all others, in religion, morals, civilization, manufacturing skill, inventive genius, naval architecture, intellectual power and literary accomplishments.

This sketch of their vain glories and ridiculous pretensions, like that of their sects and factions, is far from complete, but it may serve as a fair sample of their egotistical claims to distinction.

To each one of these vain pretensions I purpose giving a brief consideration. So innate is falsehood, and so exaggerated is self-love, in the Yankee character, that it is perfectly safe to disbelieve all their assertions, and to discredit all their claims. In religion they have reformed and improved, until all true piety has disappeared from amongst them. There is, beyond all doubt, less real religion, less true piety, amongst the Yankee race to-day, than in any other people in Christendom!

Their thousands of houses devoted, professedly to the service of religion, not only represent as many different shades of religious opinion, but are as often used for the purposes of bigotry and wrong, as for the promulgation of the peculiar tenets of the creed in whose honor they have been erected. Upon every "Sabbath," from ten thousand of what the Yankees profanely call "altars" in New England, resound the doctrines of their innumerable sects. There are preached, by the Congregationalist, the Presbyterian, the Episcopalian, the Unitarian, the Universalist and the Nothingarian, ten thousand different sermons, of which multitude of sermons true religion, the religion of the early Christians, the religion of the Bible, would not sanction ten. The staple of most of these discourses is extravagant praise of the peculiar creed of the preacher, and unmeasured denunciation of that of all the world besides. True religion makes its members kinder, truer, more patient, and more charitable to others, than other men. Are the Yankees so? Does their religion give this evidence of its truth and reality? All the world knows the contrary, and thus is proved that the Yankees have positively less religion than any other people. As in religion, so also in morals, the Yankees are sadly deficient. Here, as in religion, their pretensions are of the loftiest character. But true morality, like true religion, is evidenced and judged of by its fruits. True morality requires, amongst other things, a due observance of, and respect for, the rights, feelings and privileges of others. This is one of the first, and indispensable, tests of its existence. If Yankee morality has yielded any such fruit, it has been wholly monopolized by themselves; no one outside the pale of Yankeedom has ever been favored with any particle of this sort of evidence. On the contrary, Yankee morality, as well as Yankee religion, is as much a by-word of scorn, contempt and reproach, as ever was Punic faith! In point of civilization, if there is any particular in which they have surpassed any of the rest of the civilized world, it is a profound secret to everyone except the Yankees themselves; while in truth, honesty, kindness, charity, humanity and hospitality, generally considered as the strongest evidences, and invariable concomitants, of a high civilization, it is well known to all that they have been greatly excelled by far the larger portion of the Christian world. In ship-building the Yankees, taking advantage, very properly no doubt, of the skill of all nations, and the best models of the world, and making some alterations, additions, or other changes, have produced some good vessels, on the strength of which, with their natural egotism and arrogance, they have aspired to the title of the first ship builders of the world. It would be very difficult to name any institution of any kind, or any literary work of any character, the pure and sole result of Yankee mind or Yankee literature, now in existence, which ever has, or ever has deserved, to live for a generation. This may answer their claim to intellectual power. As to their literary productions, instead of being the original and native outpourings of their own minds, they are imitated, or pirated from the great writers of all lands.

CHAPTER EIGHT

☆ ☆ ☆ ☆

I was obliged to close, somewhat abruptly, in my last number, without having meted out full justice to Yankee prowess in the arena of literature, by the limits to which I am restricted; but I shall endeavor to complete that duty in this. As, for their own selfish ends, the Yankees had insisted upon the passage of high tariff laws, so, for the same selfish purposes, they refused a law of International Copyright. In both instances they succeeded in compassing their purposes. In both cases the advantages inured solely to their own benefit. The tariff laws fostered and supported their manufactures, while taxing heavily all the agricultural industry of the country; but the cunning Yankees escaped their share of this taxation by the very limited amount of their agricultural interests arising from the barren and sterile quality of their soil. The absence of an International Copyright permitted them to exercise their natural propensity for thieving by pirating the best literary works of Europe. In this, as in the former case, they entirely escaped any danger of retaliation.

The Yankees, themselves, were the sole and entire

source and origin of all American literature, and the very mediocrity, inferiority and worthlessness of their productions, fully insured them against all danger of reprisal. Yankee literature, in cases where it was not pilfered wholesale from foreign writers, was a trashy, vapid mixture, a dull *melange* of French frivolity, German transcendentalism and English formality, flavored and finished as opportunity served by sectarian bigotry, Puritan intolerance, and provincial ignorance. The large majority of Yankee writers produced a constant stream of books and pamphlets, of no value or importance, vapid, dull, monotonous and wearisome. Those of higher pretensions selected some distinguished English writer, and, so far as their feeble powers allowed, endeavored to imitate his style. In this, to a certain extent, they succeeded. The peculiarities of a writer's style are not very difficult of imitation, especially to the Yankees, who are gifted with the powers of imitation in a degree surpassed only by their worthy prototype, the monkey. Thus we have seen countless copyists of the singular phraseology, and wild involutions – the inversions, the obscurity and the mysticisms of Carlyle, but entirely wanting in his wonderful vigor of thought, depth and accuracy of judgment, and giant grasp of mind. So, too, have we had innumerable imitators of the graceful, flowing and finished diction of Addison, but wholly destitute of his brilliant wit, polished satire, pure morality, and elevated Christian piety. Imitators, counterfeiters, forgers in all things, and at all times, in nothing have the Yankees given more conspicuous and conclusive manifestations of their native baseness than in those contemptible, puerile, worthless productions, which they have complacently styled their "Literature." Their newspapers have been chiefly devoted to the advocacy of their doctrines, of carrying out the selfish policy of some local party, some bigoted sectarianism, or some vile proscriptive and persecuting fanaticism. Their magazines have over-flowed with nonsensical rhyme, sickly sentimentality, or mawkish love stories, more tiresome and soporific than "a twice told tale."

In the domain of invention and discovery the Yan-kees lay claim to exclusive distinction, and they amply deserve it; but the distinction is not exactly of the charac-ter they would desire. The Patent Office, at Washington, though greatly reduced in its dimensions by conflagration, yet stands an enduring monument, alike of Yankee igno-rance and stupidity, and of Yankee falsehood, baseness and fraud. There may be seen innumerable modes and specifications of inventions for all impracticable and im-possible purposes. There you may see dozens of models of "perpetual motion," plans for perfectly squaring the circle, and inventions of like character – all the emanations of the Yankee mind, and all conceived and concocted in entire ignorance of, and direct opposition to, the experience, the reason, the common sense of mankind, and the well known laws of philosophy, science and mechanics. There, too, you can find some useful inventions, but, as a general rule, they are Yankee alterations, or adaptations of the ideas and discoveries of some original thinker, some skill-ful and practical scientific mind of another race than the Yankee. Of all their lying claims to credit for original dis-coveries and inventions, the only ones that have any foun-dation in truth are to be found in the line of quack medi-cines. Here the Yankees stand truly unrivalled, and the glory is all their own! They have filled the land with patent medicines – with nostrums for the cure of every ill to which flesh is heir. Not content with Catholicons, for the prompt cure of all diseases, they have sent out special remedies for every specific disease!

If any physician of skill and experience discovered a remedy of real value, the Yankees immediately flooded the country with a worthless imitation, with counterfeit labels and certificates to ensure its being palmed off upon the people. These quack nostrums display in fair but glaring colors the native baseness of Yankee nature. Concocted of all and any materials, so they were only cheap, and could be made "to pay"; put up and vended by those who did not even profess any knowledge either of medical science or chemical principles, they were scattered recklessly through the country. That most of these nostrums were of a deleterious character is beyond question. That a large amount of human suffering, and a considerable sacrifice of human life, have been the result of this single enterprise of Yankee cupidity and Yankee inhumanity cannot be doubted. What cared they, so they succeeded in making money! Like "Margrave," in the "Strange Story," the Yankees have ever said, by their actions, more explicit than any verbal declarations – "Let all die – I will live, I will live!" What has human suffering, or the waste of human life, ever mattered to the Yankees, so they could "put money in their purse?"

I now come to manufactures, but before taking a final leave of the Yankees as inventors and quacks, I wish to add a few words to what I have already said upon these subjects. As inventors the Yankees are chiefly conspicuous for their usual selfishness and knavery; as quacks we have seen that, in addition to these amiable and characteristic qualities, they have manifested their natural inhumanity and cruelty. By the phraseology of the Patent Laws, as construed by the Yankees, no honest man could be protected in the enjoyment and the profit of his discoveries or inventions, against their interpolations and infringements. The applicant for a patent was obliged to give, under oath, an exact description of the nature and character of his work – that it had never been discovered or used by any other person; in substance, that it was an original invention or discovery of his own. An honest man could, and would, describe only what he had really invented, and no more. Here was a fine opening for Yankee "enterprise"! If he saw that the invention was one of real importance and utility – in a word, that it would "pay" – he immediately set about converting it to his own use and benefit. He added or subtracted a nail, a screw, a hinge, or altered a tube or a valve, and claimed, and, by the aid of the Yankee Patent Office officials, obtained, a patent in his own name for the invention which was really, and truly, the property of another. But it may be thought that this would avail the Yankee but little, as another knave might play upon him the same rascally game which he had played upon the original and true inventor. Not at all. Here the Yankee found an appropriate field for the exhibition of his distinguished ability.

In the description of his new invention he luxuriated in the exercise of his imagination. Although under oath, the Yankee was not to be "cabined, cribbed, confined," by any such trivial restraints as conscientious scruples. What was a lie more or less to him whose whole life was a lie? What was perjury to him whom no obligations, however indisputable, no claims, however sacred, could bind?

In his specifications, therefore, the unscrupulous and unprincipled Yankee, set forth in full, not only all that the original discoverer had invented, and all that he himself had altered and added, or taken away, but all the additions, subtractions, changes, alterations, he could imagine or divine, and boldly claimed to have discovered the whole, thus forestalling by fancy and perjury, as far as possible, all competition, and so obtained his patent.

The unraveling of the tangled web of Yankee falsehood, fraud impiety and shamelessness, is sickening, but still it must be done.

In the field of manufactures, the assumptions and pretensions of the Yankees have been pre-eminently bold and presuming. Let us examine into their claims, and we shall find them, like all the rest, equally false and unfounded. Entering upon this field after they had worn out the slave trade, the Yankees first came into competition with the manufacturers of Europe. Instantly their inferiority and incapacity became manifest. They tacitly acknowledged it themselves in their loud wailings over their failures, and their importunate supplications for a protective tariff. In this, as usual, and by the usual means, they succeeded. Aided by a tariff which amounted almost to a prohibition of European manufactures, they renewed their efforts. But even the tariff they had themselves asked for and obtained did not suffice to accomplish their purposes. Indeed, so inherent is falsehood, trickery, counterfeiting and forgery in Yankee nature, that it is doubtful whether they would not, in any event, have soon resorted to the disreputable practices for which they soon became notorious. This much, however, is certain: In the very commencement of their manufacturing career, the Yankees, finding their own productions entirely worthless and unsaleable, began that course of counterfeiting the labels, stamps and brands, and forging the trade-marks and names of the best European manufacturers, and appending them to their own inferior goods, which continues, to a great extent, to the present day. By these unworthy means, aided by the prohibitory action of the tariff, the Yankees succeeded, at last, in opening the markets of the South, at least, for the sale of their fabrics. Still, either from the yet inferior quality of their goods, or the natural proclivity to fraud and chicanery of the whole Yankee race, their productions are thrown into our markets entirely divested of all means of identifying their Yankee origin, and with forged marks, labels and stamps.

Yankee goods under the name of English broadcloth, English sheeting, English shirting, are found in every store. French cloth, de laines, ginghams, muslins, boots, hats, gloves, silks and ribbons; Italian silks and laces; German muslins and cambrics; Irish linens and lawns; English cutlery, harness, saddlery, and medicines – all made in Yankeedom – crowd our shelves in town and city, in country and village. The thread is all English thread, the sewing silk is all French sewing silk. In all finer goods the Yankees counterfeit the marks of Europe. Sheffield, Birmingham, Wolverhampton, London, Paris, Lyons, Geneva, Berlin, may be read upon all their superior fabrics. Falsely accusing the South of an incapacity for manufacturing, they have stolen, for the best of their staple productions, the names of articles of a superior quality made in the South. Their imitations, in this branch of their deception, falsehood and fraud, are marked Virginia Osnaburgs, Georgia Plains, and Louisiana Cottonades; here they forge the names of Petersburg, Milledgeville and Attakapas.

The Yankees have always said, falsely and sneeringly, that the South could not manufacture; that Southerners had no ingenuity, no skill, no industry, no perseverance. This war has demonstrated the entire falsity of these assertions. Excluded, by the blockade, from all the rest of the world, Southerners have, in two years, finally equaled all the Yankees, unrestricted in every way, and aided by protective tariffs, have effected in three-quarters of a century. Their ingenuity, skill, industry and perseverance, have supplied the army with powder, rifles, muskets, bayonets, swords, sabres, and all necessary equipments. They "have crowned our fortresses with cannon, dug from the mine since the commencement of the war." They have given hats, shoes and clothing, to the soldiers, and the people at large. They built the *Manassas*, which frightened the enemy from his propriety at the mouth of the Mississippi – the *Virginia*, which sunk or scattered their vessels at Norfolk – and the *Arkansas*, which ran the gauntlet of their whole boasted Mississippi fleet, near Vicksburg, with impunity, scattering ruin and destruction in her path. These were built under every disadvantage, and the last in the wilds of the Yazoo river, and yet they proved infinitely superior to all their Yankee competitors!

It has been said that the Yankees were the inventors of horn gun-flints and wooden nutmegs. Whether this be so or not, I do not pretend to decide positively, although the dishonesty of the proceeding raises strong presumptions in their favor; but if true, these two brilliant achievements may be considered as the only cases where their inventive ability may claim undisputed originality, and their manufacturing skill, at least, unquestioned equality with that of any other people.

We have now reviewed the claims, in their various phases and aspects, which the Yankees have so impudently put forth to distinction and superiority. Their pretensions, like themselves and their Puritan, Independent,

Cameronian and Covenanting progenitors, have proved to be in all respects, self-sufficient, unfounded, and mendacious.

Having at last, disposed of these topics, I shall return to their proper character as moralists and Christians, as illustrated in their conduct towards others. I have already mentioned that in their moral persecutions – the only kind of persecution left to the kind and gentle hearts of the Yankees by the increased enlightenment of the nineteenth century – the pious and godly Yankees made their first onslaught upon the quiet, peaceable, and unoffending society of the Free Masons.

For this they had a slight excuse, in their peculiar natures, of which they shall be allowed the full benefit. That a people notoriously too loquacious to keep a secret of their own, and so curious and inquisitive as to consider the possession of a secret by another, a wrong and injury to themselves, should hate Masonry, and endeavor to destroy it, appears by no means extraordinary, for Masonry was a secret society. This was the sole offence of the Masons. No serious charge of any improper motives, or incorrect conduct, or evil intentions, were ever alleged against that ancient fraternity. With the sole exception of the ridiculous, but characteristic and base Yankee lie about the abduction and murder of Morgan, which was never credited save by a few children, old women and idiots, even slander had ever attempted to tarnish the fair fame of the society. But the Yankees were bent upon persecution, and resolved to find a victim. In this they only partially succeeded.

Their terrible story of the death of Morgan, the groundwork and foundation of the excitement, was soon exposed in its true, falsity, and the commotion began rapidly to subside. In order to prevent Anti-Masonry from dying so speedy a natural death, and to secure to themselves some benefit from their zealous labors, for as yet they had reaped none, the Yankees, with their usual "cuteness," and unfailing want of principle, made an effort to change the character of the Anti-Masonic crusade from a pretended moral and religious, to one of a political nature. They struggled vigorously to make it a stalking-horse upon which the mighty ride into power. In this they signally failed, and then they quietly dropped the whole matter. The sincerity of their pretensions, and the truth of their charges against Masonry, are sufficiently illustrated by the two facts, which are indisputable, that there are more Masons, and more Masonic lodges, amongst even the Yankees, to-day, than at any preceding time; and that since their failure to convey Mr. Wirt into the White House at Washington, they have never made any effort either to suppress the existence, or prevent the extension, of Masonry upon their own soil!

Here the recollection of the conduct of their Puritan progenitors, in the murder of King Philip, suggests to us the very great probability that if Morgan, or anyone else, was really murdered, just preceding the outburst of Anti-Masonry, the Yankee Anti-Masons were themselves the murderers. The cases are true parallels, the motives identical, and the action in perfect keeping with Yankee character, supposing there were really any truth in the absurd story of Morgan.

In a few years the Yankees commenced their great Temperance movement. Here, for once, they had a good cause to advocate, but it is astonishing how soon a good, or a praiseworthy cause, becomes disgusting and loathsome when it has fallen under the influence and favor of

Yankee fanaticism! That the temperance cause was a good cause, and that the frightful amount of intemperance in our country was a crying evil, and well calculated to startle and alarm all worthy members of society, is undoubtedly true. By persuasion, conviction, and a just magnanimity on the part of the friends of Temperance, something has been done for the amelioration of the state of society in this respect, and much more might have been effected but for the bigotry and spirit of persecution manifested by the Yankees.

Who ever heard of persuasion, argument or magnanimity being manifested by Yankees, more especially when they believed themselves in a position where they could make use of compulsion? From the very outset of the temperance movement, the Yankees, perfectly mad, as usual, in the wildness of their fanaticism, and in full keeping with all their past history, strove vigorously to force men to become temperate by stern rebuke, severe proscription, and furious denunciation. As was customary amongst them, they soon changed this movement from a social and a moral, into a religious and sectarian contest. Every man who drank at all, though never so small the amount, of alcoholic liquors, or even wine, was denounced as unworthy of confidence and support by the immaculate Yankee temperance apostles, although he had never been known to be intoxicated during a long life of usefulness and honor, while many of those who denounced him had been, until within a very short period, of very intemperate habits, and some of them absolute and well-known drunkards. So far did these infatuated Yankees go, that they even trampled on the express command of the Saviour of mankind, when it conflicted with their fanatical doctrines. Wine was banished from their "meeting houses" at the "communion service," and various substitutes adopted in its place. What these substitutes were I am uninformed, but judging from the well-known main principle of Yankee character, and mainspring of Yankee conduct, I presume the chief one was cider. This, it is true, was as much tainted with alcohol as rum, but there was this difference in favor of the Yankees – the wine they were obliged to buy, the cider they had to sell; for the first they must pay out money, for the last they would pocket money. Be this as it may, they denounced all who dared to use wine in the Eucharist, in accordance with the command of Jesus Christ, and refused to commune with them. The natural result of such bigotry, fanaticism and intolerance, is easily anticipated. The temperance cause, so rudely checked at the outset, languished, decayed, and, so far as the Yankees are concerned, died a natural death from inaction.

CHAPTER NINE

☆　☆　☆　☆

I have now given a sufficient sketch of the Yankees and their antecedents, and traced Yankee character through all its various, but consistently infamous, phases, through Cameronian, Independent, Roundhead, Puritan and Pilgrim, down to the present time. I have portrayed in faithful colors, although with merited and just severity, the conduct and career of all these vile sectaries, and political incendiaries, until we find all their false, villainous and infamous qualities and characteristics embodied, concentrated, even surpassed, by the Yankee's. From such an ancestry we may well imagine what kind of a posterity would, necessarily, descend, and we find our anticipations not only fully realized, but greatly exceeded. A more unworthy and ignoble race, a viler, more pernicious, or contemptible rabble, never degraded the bright image of God in humanity, or desecrated the fair heritage of earth, bestowed in His beneficence. Of this, the facts heretofore stated, and hereafter to be given, being calmly and dispassionately estimated, let the truth be decided, and a just verdict awarded, by a "candid world."

In alluding to the innumerable follies, superstitions, and fanaticisms of the Yankees, I have named but a small portion, slightly sketched a few, and dwelt upon none. For this I have neither space nor time. So full is their whole history of such disgraceful records, that fully to enumerate them would require a volume; to discuss them, a library. There is one of their absurd and mischievous fanaticisms, which came into notice some thirty-five or forty years since, which demands and shall receive more especial, and particular attention. This is Abolitionism. This portentous monster, of Yankee birth and training, it is, which has been the active cause of the dissolution of the once honored Union – which has destroyed a once powerful and respected Republic– which has banded State against State, and armed brother against brother – which has caused the greatest privation, suffering and affliction, which this continent has ever known – which has already occasioned and will continue to occasion, the shedding of torrents of blood – and which has opened a fountain of hatred, a Marah of bitterness, which will not be closed or neutralized by peace, and the amenities of civil life, for a century to come. That it has been the only just and sufficient cause for the severance of the accursed Union, I do not mean to imply. As a Southerner, and a South Carolinian, I am, on the contrary, of the opinion that sufficiently satisfactory grounds for the dissolution have existed for nearly half a century, and I have been always ready and willing, and often anxious, to break the bonds which linked us with the treacherous and perfidious Yankees, at any time during the last thirty years.

Their sectional class legislation, as manifested in navigation, internal improvement and tariff laws, all unconstitutional exactions upon the South for the benefit and aggrandizement of the North, were, from their first enactments, ample cause for Southern resistance.

Still the Southerners were rich, and good humored, and patient, and might, possibly, have long continued to suffer themselves to be taxed for the support of the pauper and begging North, had not the North added to the most grievous wrongs the most aggravating insults. Then came the issue; the Gordian knot – the Union– which no skill nor statesmanship could unloose – was promptly severed by the sword. That Yankee bigotry, intolerance, persecution and hypocrisy, as manifested in their Abolition frenzy, and illustrated in the election of Lincoln, were the immediate cause of the war now raging, is beyond all question. Upon the heads of the Yankees rest all the responsibility and all the odium of this internecine strife, and they alone are answerable at the tribunals of God and man for its sufferings, its bloodshed and its crimes. In the madness of their fanaticism, upon the subject of Abolition, the Yankees, who always run mad after any fanaticism, have excelled and surpassed all their preceding exploits. In their fanatical crusade against the South, the Yankees, with their usual modesty, assumed to themselves the right and the power, to sit in judgment and pass sentence on their superiors, without a trial or a hearing. Forgetting that, even if slavery were all that in their blind bigotry they painted it, they and their ancestors were principally responsible for it, they denounced slaveholders and all in communion with them, in terms of unmeasured abuse and vilification, worthy only of Billingsgate, or Yankees, and which could hardly be applied with full justice even to murderers and pirates.

With their usual pliancy of conscience and facility of memory, they forgot to state that they, themselves, were the original negro stealers and negro traders, and omitted to tell us, if slaveholders merited such appellations, with what epithets we ought properly to designate the original Yankee slave traders and kidnappers! Indulging in their wonted impudence and arrogance, they assumed the power and the right to pass judgment upon an institution, coeval with the human race, and to denounce slavery as a great evil in morals, a terrible sin in religion! Quoting in support of their wild fantasy, a few isolated texts of the Bible, they declared that slavery was in violation of the principles of Holy Writ, and contrary to the will of the Most High. For many a long year the Southerner, thus insolently summoned before the bar of public opinion by the false-hearted and mendacious Yankee, defended his cause, weakly and unwisely, on the ground of necessity. Tacitly admitting that slavery was an evil, as charged, by the insolent Yankees, he told him that the South was not responsible for it, and was unable to remedy it. He told the Northern fanatics that the institution was first imposed upon us by the English Government, then firmly fixed and riveted by their Puritan ancestry, and that now it was not in our power to remove it without imminent danger of self-destruction. This was true as far as it went, but it was not the whole truth, nor was the position the most favorable or the most advantageous which the South was entitled to assume. Abolition fanaticism has been the occasion of this much of good, that the history and character of slavery have been fully investigated, and are now perfectly understood. The result has been the entire justification of the South, and the complete condemnation and disgrace, could so base and abject a rabble be disgraced, of the Abolition fanatics of the North. The historical part of that very Bible from which the Yankee fanatics pretended to draw their authority to wage war upon slavery – that Bible which they falsely pretend to believe – records the existence and progress of slavery from the very dawn of the creation of the race of man. In that same Bible are found the laws, regulations and commands, of the very Deity the Yankees impiously, because falsely, pretend to worship, for the guidance of masters, and the treatment, management and control of slaves. These as clearly indicate the approval of God of the institution of slavery, and as evidently contemplate its continuance through all time, as those for any other relation of life, such as parent and child, and husband and wife. Throughout the Old and the New Testament there is no law, ordinance, or command, forbidding slavery; there are many for its regulation. These were given by Moses to the people, in the immediate presence of God, and with His express sanction, as manifested by the pillar of cloud which overshadowed the Tabernacle. Those laws were never abrogated by the Saviour, nor questioned by His Apostles; nay, one of them, very unlike a Yankee fanatic, sent back a runaway slave to his master. At the very period of the sojourn of the Saviour and His Apostles, slavery, in its severest form, and to an almost incredible extent, pervaded the whole Roman world. The master held the absolute fate of the slave in his hands, and might at his own pleasure, beat, torture or slay him, unquestioned and unpunished. Yet the Saviour did not see fit to interfere with slavery as He found it in the world, and His immediate Apostles, like all His true apostles and followers ever since, followed His example, and wholly refrained from all interference with an institution of which He had expressed no disapproval.

Truly and justly has it been said, "that to find any precedent or any justification of his fanaticism, the Yankee must have a new Bible, and a new God;" and it must be an Abolition revelation, and an Abolition Deity. It has been the good pleasure of that God whom all Christendom adores, in the pages of that Revelation which every true Christian reveres, to reveal to us that, in some instances, slavery existed by His own especial interference and will, in furtherance of the wisest manner of carrying out the decrees of His providence.

The Jews, His chosen people, were enslaved more than once, sometimes this was for the punishment of their sins, or the sins of their forefathers; sometimes it was for their own benefit. When a powerful nation, they were conquered by Nebuchadnezzar, and carried as slaves to Babylon, where they remained, as a punishment, in slavery, for the space of seventy years. In their infancy as a people, they were enslaved in Egypt during the lapse of four hundred years, but this was for their benefit. They went down into Egypt a small and scanty band – Israel, his twelve sons, the Patriarchs and their families– but they increased, and multiplied, and waxed strong in slavery, and they went up out of Egypt a powerful and mighty nation. The Abolitionist Yankees, had they lived in the times, and in the dominions, of Nebuchadnezzar and of Pharaoh, would have rebelled against those monarchs, and waged war for the liberation of their Hebrew slaves, and thus endeavored their feeble utmost to defeat the decrees of the Almighty, and impiously entered, to the extent of their puny power, into a contest with Omnipotence!

Is it, by any means, certain that they are not doing so even now? But even if well assured of this, it is doubtful whether Yankee bigotry and fanaticism would cease their usual mad proceedings. They, who are notorious for giving information to the Deity, and volunteering their advice as to His action, in their long and impious prayers, would, probably, not hesitate in their frenzy to oppose His will, although made perfectly clear and indisputable to even their benighted minds. Taking into consideration the facts that slavery has always existed in the world, from the earliest ages – that it has never been forbidden, but approved by the Almighty – that it was not rebuked, but sanctioned by the Saviour – and that it was encouraged and sustained by His Apostles, one would suppose that the Yankees would be a little more reserved in their denunciations, a little more reasonable in their conduct. If they had any particle of modesty, or any shadow of reverence for anything, one would think that they might profit by the wisdom of the counsel of Gamaliel in relation to the persecution of the Disciples of Christ by the Jews, and "take heed lest in this matter they be found fighting against God." How do these bigoted fanatics know that the enslavement of the African race is not in direct accordance with the will and ordinance of Jehovah? How can they be certain that this is not for the ultimate benefit of the Africans, as was the enslavement of the Hebrews in Egypt? Or what assurance have they that it is not for punishment of the sins of themselves or their forefathers, as in the captivity at Babylon? Is there not sufficient evidence in the Bible the Yankees profess to believe, and to whose precepts they pretend to conform, for warranting the belief that African slavery should exist, that it should be perpetuated, and that it is in perfect accordance with the Divine decrees?

Is it not admitted that Ham settled Africa by all Christian peoples? Is it not acknowledged that the Africans are his descendants by all Christendom? Was not the punishment of slavery to his brethren, for himself and all his posterity, denounced, for his offences, by the Patriarch Noah, speaking in the power and the wisdom of the Most High, and by His special authority? If the Yankees do not deny these facts – facts which all the rest of the Christian world admit – what possible justification can they find, in Sacred Writ, for their mad crusade against slavery? If they deny them, then, indeed, they must needs have a new Bible and a new God! And have they not already supplied themselves with these necessary adjuncts to the cause of bigotry? That they have another God – not a new one, by any means, to them – but another than Jehovah, the God of Abraham, and of Isaac, and of Jacob, I am well aware; it is Plutus, the God of Money! and they having been occupied, many years, in revising, altering and improving the Revelation of the Almighty, it is highly probable that they have succeeded at length in providing themselves with a new Bible – not the Bible dictated and inspired by Omniscience, but the text-book and Bible of – Bigotry! It would be in perfect keeping with Yankee character, to have armed themselves with such weapons, by such means, to carry on their unhallowed crusade.

Having commenced the attack upon slavery in a perfectly characteristic style, the Yankee fanatics have carried it on in a like consistent and, to them, natural manner.

Newspapers were established to support, encourage and propagate their heresies, and put in charge of unprincipled men; worthless persons traversed the country lecturing against slavery. Pulpits resounded with the outcries of fanatical preachers against the South. Abolition societies were formed throughout Yankeedom. Into all the books with which their presses groaned, falsehoods, and slanders of slavery and slaveholders were slily insinuated, even when these very books were intended for, and in reality sent, to the Southern market. Abolition pamphlets, sermons, newspapers, almanacs, in countless numbers thronged every highway and byway of the reading world. In all these the institution of slavery, and the slaveholders, were virulently attacked and furiously denounced. The very Constitution of our forefathers, considered as a monument of wisdom, by the rest of the world, by which Southern rights were protected from outrage, and Southern property from pillage, but which put a check upon these mad enthusiasts in their wild career, was spurned, trampled, spit upon, and denounced as "a league with Death and a covenant with Hell." Fanaticism and intolerance had full license, and enjoyed, as they still do, a grand saturnalia.

In the very insanity of their zealotry, the Yankee Abolitionists, not satisfied with having belied the Bible, by pretending to find in it a sanction for their outrageous creed and abominable practices, deliberately set aside the positive commands of God, when not in accordance with their wishes, and trampled on the Decalogue, when it would have restrained their persecutions. Falsely declaring that the Bible prohibits slavery, and upon this ground refusing to hold communion with slaveholders, they forgot, or deliberately disobeyed, the express laws, written by the finger of God upon the tables of stone, which say: "Thou shalt not kill," and, "Thou shalt not steal." In the fierce ardor of their pretended love towards the slave, and their anxiety to restore him to his rights, they forgot all love, or rather became all hatred, to the master, and wholly forgot that he had any rights at all.

They commenced the systematic stealing of our slaves, and when they were pursued by the master, they coldly murdered the white owner. Their love for the black man, emblematical of their own black hearts, prompted them to any and every deed of oppression and cruelty to Southern men which did not require courage and manhood, or where they could avail themselves of the advantage of overwhelming numbers. Keenly solicitous, alike for the temporal happiness and the eternal welfare of the African, the Yankee Abolitionist, by every means of which he could avail himself, incited the ignorant slave to rob, to murder, and to run away from his master. The Yankee preachers, in their philanthropic zeal, have petitioned the United States Congress, three thousand at a time, for the suppression of slavery in the South, while, again forgetful of the Decalogue and the seventh commandment, none were moved to petition for the abolition of polygamy in Utah!

The fate of the poor slave, who was himself utterly ignorant of his very wretched condition, occupied all the time the zeal and efforts of these pious enthusiasts, while the abominations of Mormonism appear to have been considered by them as wholly unworthy of their notice. Amongst these bigoted preachers, Henry Ward Beecher who recently escaped the merited punishment of his enormities by a mob in New Jersey, through the aid of the police, stands conspicuous, not for his ability, but his infamy. He is, so far as I know, the first if not the only preacher of the Yankees, who has totally discarded all the decent observances of his profession, and openly recommended murder from the pulpit, saying "that Sharpe's rifles were the best arguments to use against the slave owners" in Kansas. I pay him the distinction of this special notice, not only on account of his own particular merit, but in deference to the claims of his family. He is the brother of that

Mrs. Harriet Beecher Stowe, who is the author of that false, malicious and infamous caricature of Southerners, and slander of the South, called *Uncle Tom's Cabin*, a work which, though quite notorious, and quite successful in the great object for which it was written – money-making – is one which no man of decent self-respect would not blush to own as his production, and which no woman but a Beecher would have written. The father of this amiable pair is Lyman Beecher, a preacher, whose excessive bigotry and intolerance drove him to Ohio, even from the bigoted and intolerant city of Boston – Boston, which, modestly calling itself the "Modern Athens," is like to ancient Athens in nothing, not even its idolatry; for while the Greek Athenians worshipped many gods, the Yankee Athenians worship only one – Gold! These Beechers are not without talent, but, from the malevolence of their natures, it has never manifested itself except in working evil to society and to humanity.

CHAPTER TEN

☆　☆　☆　☆

The Yankees, having embraced their last and wildest fanaticism, Abolition, with more than common ardor, commenced and still continue, their scheme of proselyting and propagandism with even more than their wonted intolerance, bigotry, and utter disregard of all upright or honorable principles. In addition to the means and appliances for the furtherance of their nefarious ends, heretofore stated, they endeavored, by every dishonest and sinister method, to scatter their inflammatory prints, and spread their incendiary doctrines, finding most of their Abolition publications suppressed by the Southern post offices, they resorted to the villainous plan of sending them, as wrappers, with the goods and merchandise they shipped to the South. Their unprincipled emissaries penetrated all parts of the Southern States, mingling secretly with the slaves, endeavoring to instil their vile doctrines into the minds of the negroes, and to incite them, by every means and every inducement, to the most fiendish acts of incendiarism, outrage and assassination.

These devilish emissaries, when detected, were immediately expelled from the society, and banished from the limits of the Southern States. Here the South committed a great oversight, a serious error; instead of banishing these fiendish fanatics, they should have hanged them to the nearest tree.

The professions of the Abolitionists were, in the commencement, equally false and fair. "They wished only to convince the Southern people of their error, and then leave the matter entirely in their own hands. They were very warmly interested in the welfare of the negroes, but, at the same time, they were full of kindness and affection towards their masters. They would never counsel or countenance the violation of the laws of the land, nor any infraction of the Constitution." Oh, no! immaculate, unspotted, unequaled philanthropists, they were the last persons in the world who could be guilty of such enormities! Their tender and sensitive consciences impelled them, as a bounden duty, to point out to "their Southern brethren" the sin of slaveholding, and this solemn and unavoidable duty they must needs perform!

That duty, however, once discharged, they would wash their hands of the whole affair; and, their own skirts being clear, they would leave the conduct of slavery, and the fearful responsibilities of the slaveholders, to rest between them and their Maker! Mild, charitable, pious, apostolic Abolitionists! These professions, so plausibly and persistently put forth, were like all of those of the whole race, for three centuries, entirely unfounded and utterly false. At the very time they were, with shameless hypocrisy, putting them forth to the world, they were straining every energy to induce the slaves to rise against their masters – to inaugurate a servile war in the South – to stimulate the negro to the commission of every enormity and atrocity, and to fill the whole land with outrage, conflagration and blood! These fair and false professions did not, however, long continue. They disappeared in the first years of Abolitionism.

So soon as the Abolition party saw the addition to their numbers, and the increase of their strength, which they believed the sure indications of their final success, they threw off the mask, and avowed, in unmistakable terms, their vile schemes and their fiendish intentions. They unblushingly avowed that they were "ready and willing, whenever and wherever the opportunity occurred," to put a knife into the hand of every slave to murder his master"! The Abolition fanaticism was now wide-spread and rampant, and in the wild intoxication of anticipated triumph, these disgraceful principles, which would have covered with ineffable infamy a heathen or a savage, were openly avowed, not only by the lower rabble of Yankeedom, but by their presses, their pulpits, and their Representatives in Congress! The South was given very distinctly to understand that the institution of slavery was to be confined to the States where it already existed, and finally to be "eradicated" even there. The Abolitionists openly announced "that they would not permit slavery to be introduced into any new Territory," and that "no new State, whose constitution did not prohibit it, should be admitted into the Union." This brought on the great first struggle between the North and the South, and produced the Kansas war. The right of Southern citizens to remove, with their property of every description, to any new Territory, is one beyond all reasonable doubt, but the wisdom of testing the matter in Kansas is not quite so manifest. Slavery, like everything else under the control and management of man, must submit to the teachings of experience, and be controlled by the laws of nature. It is perfectly evident that neither in location, climate, nor soil, nor in the character and nature of those who were clearly to be, in all human probability, the large majority of its inhabitants, was Kansas at all adapted, or in any way suited, to be the field upon which to try the rights of the South in the experiment of introducing slavery into a new Territory. The equal, if not superior, rights of the South to the occupancy and use of the Territories is both clear and undisputable. The Territories were all the common property of all the States, won by the expenditure of their blood and treasure in common, but not in equal proportions, the proportion, of each, paid by the South, being far greater than that paid by the North. That the South paid far the larger proportion of the money needs no argument, for she has always done so, for all governmental expenditures, since the beginning of our national history. That she bore a like unequal part of the burden, in men, is easily established. What may have been the relative amount of soldiers furnished by the North in the Revolutionary war, I do not now recollect, nor have I, at this time, any means of ascertaining; but, fortunately, I do remember the respective quotas furnished, by the North and the South, during the second war with Great Britain, and the war with Mexico, and from these we may draw a fair inference as to what was the ratio of the Yankees in men at the Revolution. In the war of 1812-1814, the South furnished 96,812 soldiers; the entire North, 58,552, making a majority in favor of the South of 38,260. The whole of the Yankee States furnished, for this war, 5,162 men, and the single State of South Carolina, 6,696, being, a majority over New England of 534.

In the Mexican war the disparity was still greater.

The North contributed 23,054; the South 53,630 – nearly double in the absolute number of men sent into the field, and in proportion to population, four times as many as the North! Of those sent by the North, Yankeedom furnished only 1,048 – Massachusetts sending 1,047; New Hampshire immortalized itself by sending one! and the other New England States none! Thus we see that both in the war of 1812 and the Mexican war, the South contributed twenty times as many soldiers as all Yankeedom! It is, therefore, fair to conclude that, even in the Revolutionary war, the Southern troops exceeded in numbers those of the North.

In point of taxation, in every shape, the inequality has been infinitely greater, for here the "cute" Yankees have managed, through cajolery and cozening, that the South should contribute not only twenty to their one, but an hundred, or a thousand! The South, having thus paid by far the larger portion, in men and money, for all the Territories which became the common property of the country, would seem to have been entitled to, at least, an equal share of them for their own benefit, and to be used at their own pleasure, and to protection therein, by the Constitution and the laws of the Federal Government, which both guaranteed these rights to the Southern, in common with all her citizens. But "no," said the mild, the pious, the benignant North; "you shall do no such thing!" There is a "Higher Law,'' said Garrison, and Phillips, and Beecher, and Greeley, "a law above the Constitution and the acts of Congress." There is an "Irrepressible Conflict," said Seward, and Yankee bigotry and intolerance soon caused his prediction to be realized. Some few Southerners had removed to Kansas, taking with them their slaves. Instantly all the Abolition hive was in commotion. Bigotry had said that slavery must not be extended, and fanaticism resolved to maintain the assertion. All Yankeedom was in a violent ferment. The Abolition press, pulpits and societies, were active and diligent. Emigration societies were formed, and the most restless and degraded of the Abolition horde were fitted out, armed and equipped with rifle and musket, and sent to Kansas by the societies, to outnumber, rob, oppress and murder quiet and peaceable Southern citizens. But in subduing the Southerners in Kansas then, as in the Confederacy now, the Yankee vandals met with but indifferent success. The Southern people, seeing the current of events, and intentions of the Yankees, went to the assistance of the slaveholders in Kansas; Yankee superiority in numbers was not sufficient to win them success in open field of battle, and all they could effect was, in their natural and craven line of conduct, a little stealing, and an occasional murder. Still, this effort of the Yankee Abolitionists was not wholly unproductive of some of the characteristic vices and evils, which seem inevitably to attend upon all the experiments of fanaticism.

In Kansas, during the strife, there sprung into malign existence the infamous name and practices of Jayhawkers. There rose into notoriety the ignoble villains, Montgomery and Jim Lane, and the vulgar ruffian "Ossawatamie," or "Old John Brown." There originated the germ of the same John Brown's murderous raid into Virginia, and his cold-blooded cruelties and murders at Harper's Ferry. This was the second scene in the Abolition drama which had opened in Kansas. But the plans of the principal actors had now changed; their tactics were altered entirely. In Kansas, the Yankees had proposed to themselves the congenial task of robbing and destroying Southerners, by overwhelming numbers, it is true, but still in a manner somewhat open, and a character with some specious pretensions to manliness, but at Harper's Ferry everything was to be done in darkness, in secrecy, and in entire concealment; robberies and conflagrations, murders, outrages and assassinations, were all to be confined to the hours of night! The hellish project failed, in a great measure; its instruments were mostly shot, or captured and punished more or less; and Old John Brown fell into the hands of Virginia and Governor Wise, and was hanged.

These impressive and instructive lessons were not wholly lost upon the Southern people. They began to see and appreciate the position they would occupy should this vile and unscrupulous rabble of Abolition ever obtain power to carry out their wicked and pernicious designs. It was well that the South was aroused, for the time was rapidly approaching when to have been found sleeping upon their posts would have proved irretrievable disaster and utter ruin to her and to her cause. The Abolitionists had long been striving for the attainment of power commensurate with their fanatical and destructive designs. For this they had labored day and night, in season and out of season, by all means however grovelling and debased; and this power they had, to a considerable degree acquired. Town by town, county by county, State after State, they had brought into their ranks, until the whole North had submitted to their sway. Their power and influence were manifested in the passage of what they called "personal liberty" acts, by the legislatures of all of the Northern States. These "personal liberty bills" were for the protection and security of the runaway slave, and imposed, in most cases, the punishment of fine and imprisonment upon the master who dared to seek for the restoration of his property. They were in direct violation of the Constitution, the laws of Congress, and the decisions of the Supreme Court of the United States. They were complete "nullification," and they were carried into operation. They amounted, essentially, to a destruction of the Constitution and a dissolution of the Union. In the greater part of these States laws were enacted refusing the use of the legal prisons of the State to the officers of the United States for the safe keeping of refugee slaves whom they had captured.

But all this power, and it will be readily perceived that it was a tremendous one, did not satisfy the Yankees. It had proved insufficient to enable them to carry out, with entire success and triumph, their devilish enterprises in Kansas and in Virginia. The aid of the State power, and the assistance of the State Governors, had enabled them to do much evil – to inflict many injuries, and perpetrate many wrongs and outrages upon the South, but the extent of this power was too limited, and its field of operations too confined, to afford a proper arena for the display of their infernal ability, and the full accomplishment of the fiendish objects contemplated and proposed by their evil and malevolent genius. No more contracted area than all the States of the whole Union would satisfy their unlimited ambition; no power less extensive than that of the whole Federal Government would answer their unmeasured requirements; no influence lower, or less potent, than that of the President of the United States would enable them to realize, in full fruition, all the ferocious plans of their diabolical infatuation. They determined to seize the reins of the Federal Government, to take the control of the political destinies of the whole country into their own hands – to fill Congress with their creatures, and place their puppet in the White House.

They resolved to make a desperate struggle for the

possession of all the influence, the *prestige* and the power, which attach to the name of the Government; they spared no means, neglected no appliances, omitted no efforts, to secure the victory, and they succeeded. Abraham Lincoln, their candidate, their thorough proselyte, their zealous partisan and friend, was elected, by a minority vote, President of the United States. But he was the last one ever to be elected to that once august office. Buchanan was the last actual President, and Lincoln is the last President elect of the old United States. Others may bear the title, perhaps, but no one will ever again exercise official power or authority over all the territory once embraced in the limits of the United States. The Abolitionists succeeded in electing their candidate, but they were not destined to reap the anticipated fruits of their victory.

The Yankees' first wild cry of exultation was scarcely uttered when they began to perceive that they had, in reality, but little ground for triumph and gratulation. Scarcely had they raised the cup, and tasted the first delicious flavor of power, when it was dashed from their lips, and shattered to atoms. When the election of Lincoln was ascertained to be beyond a doubt, South Carolina at once seceded from the Union; she was soon followed by others, until she, and Georgia, Florida, Alabama, Mississippi, Louisiana, Texas, Arkansas, Missouri, Virginia, North Carolina, Tennessee and Kentucky, had quietly but firmly cut off their connection with the old Union, and formed amongst themselves an independent association, which is known by the title of the Confederate States.

They endeavored to make a just and equitable settlement with the Government at Washington, and to withdraw in peace. The miserable and disgraceful shuffling, duplicity and falsehood of Lincoln and his unprincipled

Cabinet, and their final open and unquestionable treachery, are familiar to us all, and are known to the world. The result was the taking of Fort Sumter by South Carolina, and the commencement of open war. The Abolitionists stood aghast at the unexpected result of their own handiwork.

The whole result for which they had toiled, and intrigued, and lied, and sinned, for nearly half a century, had slipped through their fingers in the very hour of their fancied triumph and security. Those very Southern States which they had so long ruled unjustly and oppressively, and which they had fondly hoped they should now be able to rule absolutely, and at their pleasure, they found, to their terror and amazement, that they were not to rule at all. That the only way by which they could govern one man in, or one acre of Southern soil, was war – and a war where victory was by no means certain to be in their favor, and where a bitter and tremendous struggle, with great suffering and loss, even on their side, was well assured. Buchanan's term of office expired, and it became necessary that their champion, and the exponent of their doctrines, should be inaugurated.

Then was seen, for the first time in history, the elected Chief Magistrate of a powerful people cravenly and sneakingly slipping in disguise into the capital of the country, to assume the reins of government! Then was seen, for the first time in the history of this country, that same Chief Magistrate, in abject terror of his life, inaugurated into his high office under the countenance and protection of shining bayonets, gleaming swords and loaded cannon. What a sad spectacle for the contemplation of the admirer of republics, and the lovers of free governments!

But the shameful scene is over, and by the aid of a

disguise, and a hireling soldiery, Lincoln has become President of such portions of the old United States as are willing to acknowledge his sway. But what shall he, and his wild, mad, disappointed faction do now? The alternative lies between a peaceable release of all claim to power or authority over the Southern States, or a bloody and protracted war. The conclusion to which he and they would naturally come need not have been doubtful. That a horde of wild fanatics, whose appropriate motto would be, from their very origin, "rule or ruin," should decide in favor of war was perfectly natural, and indeed inevitable. Without war they must quietly yield up their power to tax, to oppress, and to persecute the South. Rather than relinquish, for all time to come, these dear delights, let blood flow in torrents, and treasure be wasted like water!

In perfect keeping, and entire consistency with all their past history, and that of their whole race, the Yankees chose war. What to them were the rights of others, when they stood in the way of their fanaticism? What to them was taxation, or death in the field of battle? They would cunningly avoid the one, and cravenly shun the other. These evils were for others – not for them; were they not the "cute Yankees"?

The war inaugurated by their selfishness and arrogance is now raging. In my next number I purpose to show how they have prospered in it.

CHAPTER ELEVEN

☆　☆　☆　☆

In the last number we have seen the success of Yankee fanaticism in the dissolution of the Union, the overthrow of the Great Republic, and the inauguration of a tremendous civil war. These deplorable results are due to Yankee bigotry and intolerance alone. The Yankees have won the just meed of the scorn, the contempt and the hatred of the whole, civilized world, and the abhorrence of posterity for all succeeding time. They have set the world on fire, and will be remembered with Erostratus! Branded by a history, blackened in every page by the records of disgraceful achievements, they have succeeded, at last, in winning an odious celebrity, and damned themselves to an infamous immortality which totally eclipses the turpitude of their worthy brother, Benedict Arnold, and must greatly mitigate the self reproach, and alleviate the remorse, of Judas Iscariot.

Having resolved upon the subjugation of a people over whom they had no shadow of just claim to any authority, the Yankees, with their invariable hypocrisy, sought to justify their violent and despotic conduct by pretensions and assertions equally specious and fallacious. They would, if possible, hoodwink the world, and make it believe that their cause, instead of being one of aggression and oppression, was that of order and legal right. They were not plunging the country into all the horrors of a terrible internecine war for the empty bauble of power, or the ignoble ends of gain, but for the "Constitution as it is," and the "Union as it was"! Doubtless, when they found they could gain no more, this would, for the present, have satisfied them; for, in truth, the "Constitution," by their malpractices and State laws, had become a mere dead letter, and the "Union," by their knavery, was made only one broad field for their exactions, extortions and peculations. In addition, they were the ostensible defenders of the "honor of the National Flag"! This, like the former, was a false and unfounded pretension. The Flag for which they professed such devoted affection was not surrounded by any prestige of glorious association. Adopted by Congress, in 1818, it had never floated over any field for the maintenance of the honor of the country, or the defence of human rights. Its only claims to distinction were the somewhat doubtful glories of the Florida, the Black Hawk, and the Mexican wars – doubtful, because the causes in which they were gained were of rather questionable right, justice and magnanimity.

It was truly in fine keeping with their whole history that the Yankees should be the people to precipitate this unjust and unnatural war. Their native home, New England, had been the source of, or the efficient agent, in causing all the rebellions, insurrections and civil strife, which have dishonored our country's character. There arose the "Shay's Rebellion," the "Dorr Insurrection," and the "Hartford Convention," whose now well ascertained purpose was to organize an armed resistance to the Government of the United States, which treasonable design was only prevented from manifesting itself openly by the promptitude of the United States in concluding a precipitate treaty of peace, conceded to the clamors of the North at the expense of the cause for which the war was begun, the dignity of the Government, and the rights of the people. Resolved upon an act of baseness, in bringing on a civil war, the Yankees, by a fatality we might consider singular, were it not characteristic of, and in entire keeping with, their invariable course throughout their entire history, were obliged, by their natural proclivity to degradation, to superadd to the act itself any available accessories of disgrace. The doctrine of State Rights had been carried into effect in the enactment of the so-called, "Personal Liberty bills," by everyone of the Yankee States, and the Federal Constitution and laws set at defiance. The State of Massachusetts, the centre and heart of New England, the seat of the "Modern Athens," the very soul of Yankeedom, and the hotbed of all fanaticism and superstition, had not only enacted a "Personal Liberty bill," but had passed a series of "Joint Resolutions," still, so far as I am informed, unrevoked, declaring that "when Texas came into the Union, Massachusetts went out." Texas did come into the Union, and according to her own resolve, Massachusetts was out – had in fact, seceded.

In addition to all this, the Hartford Convention, which had assembled at Hartford, in the State of Connecticut, on the 15th day of December, 1814, had adopted a report, of which the following paragraph forms a portion:

In cases of *deliberate*, dangerous and palpable infractions of the Constitution, affecting the sovereignty of a State, and the liberties of the people, *it is not only*

the right, but the duty, of each State to interpose its au-
thority for their protection in the manner best calcu-
lated to secure that end. When *emergencies* occur which
are either *beyond* the reach of *judicial* tribunals, or too
pressing to admit of the delay incident to their forms,
States, which have *no common umpire*, must be *their*
own judges, and execute their own decisions.

Here are laid down, by the Yankees themselves,
and in terms as explicit and emphatic as the most ardent
States Rights man or Secessionist could desire, the very
doctrines of State Sovereignty and Secession which the
South has ever believed and maintained, and for which she
is now battling in the field. To justify their vindictive and
unrighteous war upon the South, it was necessary for the
Yankees, with characteristic inconsistency, to act in direct,
opposition to their own professed principles, in open violation of the teachings of their own example, and, by their
shameless tergiversation, to stultify themselves before the
world. To these, and other acts correspondingly ignoble
and degrading, they did not hesitate to resort. They initi-
ated, and still conduct, the war in a spirit of bitter malignity, of thieving avarice, of wanton destruction, of shameless outrage and unbounded cruelty, totally unworthy of a
civilized people – unknown in the annals of modern war,
and which would reflect shame and disgrace upon heathen
Caffres of Africa, or the brutalized Bushman of Australia.
To increase the bands of armed hirelings they were raising
for the slaughter and subjugation of a free people, they im-
pressed or inveigled into their ranks all of the ignorant,
pauper, and criminal emigrants from Europe, and emptied
their jails and penitentiaries! Professing to the South, and
to Europe, that, whatever the result of the war, the institution of slavery should not be interfered with, or in any man-

ner altered, they have, from the very outset, stolen our slaves and appropriated their labors to their own benefit, exacting, at the same time, and in the severest manner, the utmost possible amount of that labor. Pretending that they would respect private property, they have, in all cases, greedily stolen what they could convert easily to their own use, and wantonly destroyed what they could not take away. In a spirit of vandal recklessness they have burned private dwellings, pillaged and destroyed private and public libraries, and without any military necessity, wasted and desolated the country wherever they have passed, with heartless and savage barbarity. In the face of their solemn assurances to Europe, by Seward, Adams and Dayton, Lincoln, in his Proclamation of September, endorsed and enforced as far as he could by that of the 1st of January, has announced emancipation, instant and unlimited, of all the slaves in the South.

True it is, as has been well said by some of the English papers, this is mere *brutem fulmen*, and might just as wisely and effectually have been extended to Brazil and to Africa, as confined to the Confederate States, but it shows the immeasurable falsehood and baseness of the Yankee character and Government, and displays, in their true colors, their bitter animosity and implacable hatred towards our country and our people. From the first despotic commencement, in Baltimore, the Yankees have observed neither truth, nor faith, nor justice, nor decency.

They have trampled upon all laws, and made the tyrannical will of a military dictator, wherever their forces have been in the ascendancy, the sole legislative and judicial arbiter. Free and unoffending citizens have been arrested, in the day and in the night, without legal warrant, and hurried from their homes to some military Bastile, where they have remained incarcerated for months, not only without trial, but without accusation, but merely on the suspicion of their entertaining Southern sympathies!

Women, of education and refinement, have, in the same lawless manner, been long imprisoned in houses, inconvenient, unhealthy, and without comfort, exposed at all times, and generally under their close *surveillance*, to the insults of a base, licentious and unprincipled soldiery. Even children have been arrested in the streets, and plundered of their toys, or their apparel, because they either did, or were supposed to, display the colors of the South. What a holy horror have the Yankees manifested of the stars and bars of our flag, and the gray color of our soldiers' uniforms!

These autocratic proceedings, first enforced against Southerners, with the sanction and applause of the North, by the Lincoln despotism, were soon extended to their own citizens. This, continued and increased to the present time, has begun to excite some alarm amongst the Yankees themselves. They are beginning to perceive that in the effort to usurp the liberties of the South, they have raised up a power which has stripped them of their own. They will appreciate this more fully hereafter. Liberty, law, and constitutional government have disappeared from the North forever. A stern and grinding despotism now rules, and will long continue to rule, that abject and degraded people. In this we, of the South, can feel but little interest. A population so willing to bow to the power, and lay their dearest rights at the feet, of a fanatical and despotic buffoon, in order that they may be enabled to gratify their unappeasable hatred, and glut their immeasurable avarice, in the enslavement and plunder of a free people, can claim but little sympathy in their bondage, from any one, and least of all from the South.

The infamous notoriety won by the North in the atrocities which have characterized their conduct of this war is, by no means, to be confined to the subalterns, or the rabble of the Yankee army. In the eternal shame and disgrace of their innumerable savage enormities, their wholesale burglaries, their arsons, their rapes, and their murders, their Generals and Commanders-in-Chief share in all the disgrace, and will participate in all the obloquy, which history and posterity will award to their crimes, with the lowest of their subordinates. Amongst these the lying Pope, in his orders in Virginia, and the assassin McNeill, in his murders in Missouri, stand in a light somewhat unenviably conspicuous; but high above them all, the Beast Butler, in his reign of terror in New Orleans, has attained an eminence of infamy which dwarfs their minor claims to indelible disgrace into comparatively pigmy dimensions. To the proceedings of this unmitigated moral monster, this modern Polyphemus, I must give a somewhat particular attention. To compare him to Suwarrow or Haynau would be the wildest extravagance of flattery. He commenced his disgraceful career in the city of New Orleans by the cold-blooded murder of Mumford, which remains, inexplicably, unavenged by our Government to the present time. The infamous order which has forever associated his name with those of the vilest and most degraded, of all the human monsters who have disgraced their kind, appeared speedily after his occupation of the city. In order to do full justice to the enormities of this human Brute, I shall avail myself of a portion of the Message of the Governor of Louisiana to the Legislature of the State, where they are forcibly and eloquently depicted:

In a short time the enemy entered [New Orleans], and its General commenced a career of brutality and ingenious villainy to which no parallel can be found in the history of conquered cities. Soon the celebrated order was issued, inviting his soldiery to the gratification of the most beastful lusts upon our noble-hearted women. The abhorrent disgust spontaneously expressed by the civilized world at this brutal ruffianism, extorted a lame apology and impotent justification of the outrage, but his subsequent actions evince that it was the natural emanation of a mind capable only of the vilest thoughts, and guided by the lowest instincts of a depraved nature. The history of his despotic domination over our fellow citizens of New Orleans stands out as a beacon light to warn other communities that destruction is preferable to such humiliation, and to justify to the world the righteousness of resistance to a nation whose Rulers and Generals transplant to the nineteenth century the maxims of conduct which were thought to have been buried among the records of heathenish antiquity.

You will find on our recovery of the capital evidences of the same vandalism. The majestic statue of the revered examplar of resistance to tyranny, with which the liberality of your predecessors had adorned the State House, has been abstracted, and the valuable library, the accumulation of successive years of judicious expenditure, has been partially destroyed, and the residue removed. The doors of the penitentiary were opened by these avengers of desecrated laws, and the whole of the convicts were turned loose and invited to become volunteers in their crusade for the re-establishment of the Union and the supremacy of law. Some accepted the invitation, and joined the ranks of their fellows in the Federal army. Others refused indignantly, and avoided compulsory service by flight. A large number have been carried to New Orleans and imprisoned for their refusal.

Spoliation of private property has been systematically inculcated among their needy soldiery, and here, as elsewhere in our country, the costly furniture and ornaments of private residences have been purloined, and despatched with eager haste to adorn the halls of pauper adventurers. The transparent veil of war for the restoration of the Constitution and the Union, with which the Government and followers of Lincoln have vainly endeavored to conceal their designs, has been penetrated at last even by a portion of their own subjects, and the truth seems about to dawn upon them, that in the effort to destroy our liberties, they have madly lost their own. What sacrifices shall we not endure rather than be reunited in a Government which has countenanced such atrocities, and has made a once honored republic the reproach of the world!

That all these and many other enormities, such as compelling planters to divide their crops with his brother, Ar. J. Butler, or to have their negroes driven off, and their homes and property burned and wasted, the robbery of the citizens of their gold and silver, their bills of exchange, and other commercial representatives of money, and their remittance to the North in his own name and for the enrichment of himself; and the systematic embezzlement of the commissary and other stores of his own Government, were practiced by this hoary reprobate is indisputable. It is even vouched for by the letters of his Yankee confreres who were residents of New Orleans during the time of his domination. Yet, in defiance of the public opinion of the civilized world, this same Butler, reluctantly superseded at the latest, in compliance with the indignant remonstrances of the representative of the French Government, is received in New York city with an ovation, and the Yankee

Congress, insensible of shame and of decency alike, endorse all his villainous conduct, and fully participate in, while they in no degree diminish the quantity or the quality of his utter infamy, by passing a vote of thanks to this vile murderer, debauchee and marauder.

From the outbreak of the war, the Yankees have been vainglorious and boastful of wonderful and gallant feats which they "were going" to perform. Their bravado, like that of all braggadocios, has been most ridiculously belied by their constitutionally craven conduct.

All the hard fighting of this war, and all the bravery shown, has been done, and exhibited, by the people of the West, who are as naturally brave as the Yankees are naturally cowards. The Yankees have placed their confidence in their "chariots and their horsemen" alone. They have not remembered that "the battle is not always to the strong." They have trusted to overwhelming numbers, and the power given to them by the use of their only god – Money – forgetting that "The Lord He is God, and that He ruleth in the hosts of Heaven and in the armies of earth." With their great Anaconda they were to "crush out the rebellion in ninety days"; but four times ninety days have elapsed, and the "rebellion" is not "crushed" out, but the Anaconda is. In the contraction of its huge coils for the crushing operation, it came in contact with a resistance from Southern fire and Southern steel, at Manassas, at Columbus, at Corinth, at Richmond, at Fredericksburg, at Vicksburg, and many other places, which not only astonished the crushers, and prevented the crushing, but pretty effectually scotched the snake! In almost every battle the Yankees have either, as at Manassas, marched away from the field, before the fight, to the sound of our guns, or if they awaited the first shock, have been scattered like sheep by our gallant soldiery, leaving the foreign and Western troops to bear the heat and burden of the day, and to fight out the war which Yankee fanaticism had begun. On the land, though usually greatly outnumbered, we have in a large majority of our battles defeated the enemy. They have never won any success, unless when they were at least three or four to one, and even in some of these unequal conflicts we have been victorious. On the water, the Yankees' own chosen and boasted field, having no Navy, we have had but little opportunity to try conclusions with them; still, I imagine, they retain no very flattering memories of the exploits of the ram *Manassas*, the *Virginia*, the *Arkansas*, and of the *Sumter* and the *290*, or *Alabama*; and now let them look out for the *Florida*. With their tremendous army, which they boast of as containing over a million of men – with an immense navy in their hands, and none to oppose them – with an expenditure of a thousand millions of dollars, already squandered, and more than a thousand millions of dollars already appropriated, the Yankees have effected nothing towards the accomplishment of their great end – the subjugation of the South.

In the meantime, the disgrace of their Government, in the Cabinet, has been more complete than that of their armies in the field. With the mingled whining and bullying of a braggart and a coward, the Yankee Government, in terrible fear that England or France might sometime render us that justice due alike to us and themselves, by recognition or intervention, have endeavored to stave off the dreaded evil by pitiful appeals to amity and friendly existing relations, and contemptible threatenings of vengeance in case of interference; they would then not only subdue us, which they cannot now do, but would, at the same time, fearfully punish both Great Britain and France! Miserable, shameless Yankees, at all times alike contemptible and revolting! England and France have both shown an unfair preference in favor of the Yankee Government, by denying us our just rights, in accordance with their own established usage, and their own construction of International Law. Not content with this, the Yankees threaten them with condign punishment should they ever presume to right the wrong! To gain an advantage over the South the Yankees humiliated themselves by voluntarily, and unasked, yielding their assent to the Paris treaty relative to privateers, which in the hour of their pride they had refused. But this was not to be their only humiliation in the eyes of Europe. In the mad presumption, so truly Yankee in its character, Wilkes had insulted the British flag, and taken from under its protection the Commissioners of the Confederate States. The act was an act of piracy, but all Yankeedom was in an ecstacy of joy and jubilation; Congress applauded, and the Yankee Secretary of the Navy complimented Wilkes, and the city of New York *feted* him. For a short time Wilkes, the Yankees, and their Government were in all their glory. But their triumph was of brief duration. All England was in a tempest of indignation, and the partial Government was compelled to act justly, promptly and vigorously. The Yankees would have temporized, but this was not permitted. Finally, after all their boasting, the prisoners so gloried over were humbly restored to a British deck, and Seward, conscious of the absurd and ridiculous position of himself and his Government, promulgated a long-winded and rambling letter of explanation, which concluded with the ludicrous statement that "the prisoners were restored in conformity with established American precedent and usage"! If so, why were they ever imprisoned, or why not released until peremptorily demanded? But all the world understands the full merits of the case. The Yankees yielded to fear what they refused to justice. Never was the Prime Minister, even of the most petty German State, so humiliated, so degraded, so trampled on.

CHAPTER TWELVE

☆ ☆ ☆ ☆

War, like intoxication, whether that of alcohol or gambling, always tears away the veil with which interest, habit, or hypocrisy, have induced men to shroud and conceal their true characters and natural propensities, and displays the real individuality of the person in genuine colors and natural proportions. It has thus unmasked the Yankee, in the present conflict, no less completely than it did in those of his Puritan progenitors, whether with Europeans or Indians. While making themselves, by their cowardice and pusillanimity, in the affairs of privateering and the *Trent*, the laughing-stock of Europe, they were reaping an abundant harvest of undying shame and reproach by their perfidious and savage conduct of the war in America. Our brave privateers who had unfortunately fallen into their hands, were unfeelingly, and in the gratification of an inhuman cruelty, exhibited in fetters; marched manacled through the streets to cater to the base passions of a vile rabble; thrust into loathsome dungeons like felons, and threatened with the gibbet! This threat would, undoubtedly, have been carried out, but for the consequences to their pet, Col. Corcoran, and some others, fortunately in our hands at the time, by these same Yankees who have been the most wholesale privateers of all Christendom, and who are, many of them, even now luxuriating in the privateering spoils of their fathers!

As one, amongst innumerable other instances in which the Yankees have manifested an entire destitution of honesty, and a fair sample of their morality, may be cited their persevering efforts to flood our country with counterfeit Confederate money. This base proceeding they, instead of any endeavor at concealment, which an instinctive consciousness and shame of guilt which generally dictates even the basest of men in their disreputable career, the Yankees, with unblushing effrontery, boldly proclaim to the world. Read the following article, cut from a late Mobile *Register*:

> Yankee Honesty. – Counterfeiting is shamelessly avowed and published to the world at the North. In *Harper's Weekly* (Jan. 10) – a paper which pretends to some decency – we find the following advertisement:
>
> *Confederate (Rebel) Money.* – Fac simile Treasury Notes, so exactly like the genuine that where one will pass current the other will go equally as well. Five hundred dollars in Confederate Notes of all denominations, sent by mail, postage paid, on the receipt of $5, by W. E. Hilton, 11 Spruce street, New York.

That W.E. Hilton is a consummate scoundrel is an unquestionable fact, and that the Harpers are but little better is a very fair inference. In connection with the above extract from *Harper's Weekly*, it is quite refreshing to peruse in the Yankee histories of the Revolutionary war, their fierce and bitter reprobation and denunciation of the

British for their attempts to depreciate the American cur-
rency by the surreptitious circulation of spurious Conti-
nental money. The pious indignation and holy horror of
the Yankee historians are unbounded! But this, and even
their enormous plunderings of their own Government, to
the amount of millions, could not at all satiate the Yankee
cravings of avarice, nor check their innate proclivity to
knavery. Besides their wholesale robberies of the Southern
and the Northern Governments, they indulge themselves
in their wonted avocation, minor peculation, even at the
expense of their own sick, and wounded soldiery. See the
annexed article:

> Yankee Like. – The New York *Tribune* says it is
> currently reported that large bundles and bales of new
> bandages and lint, contributed by the people for poor
> wounded soldiers, have been sold to paper makers at Dal-
> ton, Mass.

These extracts must be admitted as unquestionable
evidence, as against Yankees and Abolitionists, for they
are taken from papers, one under the editorial control of
Raymond, and the other under that of Greeley – two as
genuine Yankees, and as bigoted and fanatical Abolitionists, as can be produced in all New England. In conformity
to their natural and inherent propensity for imitation,
especially in actions of very questionable reputation, the
Yankees followed the example of Great Britain in another
disreputable and unjustifiable practice, of which no one
ever complained more lugubriously than they did when it
was enforced against themselves. The British, considering
the colonists "rebels" against the majesty of the British
Empire, refused, for a long time, to release their captives

upon any terms whatever. The Yankee newspapers of the time, and all their histories since, teem with doleful descriptions of the sufferings of the republican prisoners in the enemy's jails and prison hulks! So the Yankees, affecting to look upon Confederate prisoners as "rebels" against their majesty, determined not to liberate them at all, either on parole, or in exchange. They adhered to this unfeeling decision until the fate of war had thrown the larger number of prisoners into the hands of the Confederates.

Then the Yankee Government, driven, at last, by the sufferings of its own soldiers, and their loud and bold remonstrances, as well as those of their friends and relatives, was forced to abandon the position so inhumanly assumed. It still pretended to consider the Confederates as rebels, and itself as the legitimate and only Government, and, being a persistent stickler for forms and appearances when in accordance with its interests, consented only to an "informal" exchange. Before the formalities of that exchange could be completed, the chances of war, by the fall of Fort Donelson, had thrown the balance of prisoners considerably in its own favor. Instantly, with wonted treachery and bad faith, it refused to fulfill its agreements, and no exchanges were, for a considerable time, effected! The career of the Yankees has been distinguished, in its whole course since the commencement of this war, by unprovoked destruction of property, and inexcusable waste of life.

Even as I write, new instances of their destructive and barbarous proceedings are furnished me, in great abundance, by the daily papers, from which I have already made, and shall continue to make extracts. Not content with the wanton, lawless burnings of dwellings, and other property, by their unbridled soldiery, it has been encouraged and sanctioned by their Generals, who by their official orders and personal participation, have lent their countenance to these dastardly crimes. See the order of Brig, Gen. Mitchell:

Headquarters Post,
Nashville, Tenn., Jan. 9, 1863

Special Order No. 9. – I. In consequence of the wanton destruction of a locomotive and construction train upon the Nashville and Chattanooga Railroad this day, by one Richard McCann and Thomas Kilkird, leading a gang of outlaws, the property of those men will be destroyed. Col. Moore, 85th Illinois volunteers, will proceed immediately with his regiment along the line of the Railroad to the houses of the persons above named, and destroy their houses, barns, fences and other property susceptible of destruction upon their respective grounds, by fire or any other means at his command.

II. It is hereby announced that the property of all parties engaged in interrupting the workings of the Nashville and Chattanooga Railroad, or other railroads in this vicinity, or of the passage of the Cumberland river, will be treated in like manner with the property mentioned in the above order, so far as it is in the power of the General commanding at this post so to treat it.

III. All property of any kind belonging to any rebel or rebel sympathizer, found within one mile of the locality of any similar outrage perpetrated upon the line of railroad, or on the banks of the river in this vicinity, will be destroyed in the manner described.

By order of Brig. Gen. R.B. Mitchell, commanding post.

John Pratt, A.A.G.

The "one Richard McCann and Thomas Kilkird" here mentioned in the first section of this order, are officers in the service of the Confederate States. They were engaged in breaking up the communications of the enemy and arresting his supplies, things fully sanctioned by usage in the wars of the most enlightened nations, and practiced by them at all times. The "gang of outlaws" were Confederate soldiers. Yet the property of these officers is wantonly destroyed by order of this Yankee General, for the crime of obeying the commands of their own Government.

But even this does not satisfy the destructive propensities of General Mitchell. By the third section of this order the property of all within a mile of the place, on railroad or river, where the Confederate forces may dare to interfere with His Highness' convenience, is to be ruthlessly destroyed, although they be entirely innocent of any complicity with, or knowledge of, the matter, unless they are recreants and traitors to their country!

In murdering, the Yankees are equally discontented with being confined to unarmed and unoffending men, and have, with the sanction of the presence, and in obedience to the orders, of no less than a field officer, commenced the cold-blooded and cowardly assassination of helpless women and children, as seen in the following article:

Murders in Missouri. – The Jackson *Crisis* publishes the following stateinent on the authority of a gentleman direct from Missouri:

Col. Wm. R. Pennick, in command of a regiment of militia, not long since left St. Joseph with his troops in search of "bushwhackers," and having reached Clay county, arrested Chas. Pullins, who left Buchanan in company with Capt. Gibson for the Southern army. Pullins was taken to Liberty, a mock trial was gone throughwith, and he was condemned to be hung. He offered to prove that he was a regularly enlisted Confederate soldier, but was denied the privilege, and accordingly hung. After hanging Pullins, Pennick proceeded two or three miles further, and found two men sitting in a widow's door. He asked them if they knew of the whereabouts of any bushwhackers. Upon being answered in the negative he proceeded a short distance, when he was attacked and his regiment repulsed by men concealed in the brush. Pennick immediately returned to the widow's house, hung the two men he had seen there and burned the house. Crossing the river into Jackson county, nominally in search of Quantrel, some of his men arrested a boy who was taking clothes to Quantrel's command. They went to the house of the boy's mother, who was a widow, seized and hung both her and her son. This man, Pennick, disgraces the position of Grand Master of the Masonic fraternity in Missouri.

Firing upon hospitals where the yellow flag is flying, and bombarding towns without notice, are savage but common Yankee practices.

Conduct so gratuitously cruel, so horribly atrocious, has never been witnessed in any civilized nation, even in the most vindictive conflicts of civil war, since the times of Puritan domination in England, or the campaign of their worthy competitor for the prize of eternal infamy, the Duke of Alva, in the Low Countries. Even the least corrupt of the tools of Lincoln, it appears, cannot long serve his Government, or associate with his other instruments of tyranny and violence, without contracting a large portion of their mendacity, and much of their natural baseness. Witness the following order, recently issued by Gen. Rosecrans:

Retaliation. – The following (says the *Rebel Banner* of the 20th) is the order of Gen. Rosecrans, under which the Confederate officers captured in the battles near Murfreesboro have been sent to Alton, Ill., to be kept in close confinement:

Headquarters Department Cumberland,
Murfreesboro, Jan. 6, 1863

General Order No. – The General commanding is pained to inform the commissioned officers of the Confederate army taken prisoners by the forces under his command, that, owing to the barbarous measures announced by President Davis in his recent proclamation, denying paroles to our officers, he will be obliged to treat them in like manner. It is a matter of regret to him that the rigor appears to be necessary. He trusts that such remonstrances as may be made in the name of justice, humanity, and civilization, will reach the Confederate authorities as will induce them to pursue a different course, and thereby enable him to accord to their officers the privileges which he is always pleased to extend to brave men, even fighting for a cause which he considers hostile to our nation, and disastrous to human freedom.

By command of General Rosecrans,
C. Goddard A.A.A.G.

In this order Gen. Rosecrans, who has hitherto occupied a rather more respectable place in public opinion than the balance of the Yankee officers, has degraded himself to their level. In designating the proposed measures announced in the proclamation of President Davis, as "barbarous," he was guilty of deliberate falsehood, for he was fully aware that they were in just retaliation of the well-known murders and other enormities of the "Beast Butler" in New Orleans. This is plainly and explicitly stated by President Davis in his Proclamation. This order of Rosecrans is in fact, an endorsement and approval of the course of Butler in New Orleans, and justly makes its author a participant in his degradation and infamy. But the Government of Lincoln is not to be surpassed in baseness even by the basest and most zealous of its subjects. Not satisfied with the operation of their paper blockade, that vile despotism, in violation of all the usages of war, and in a cruel, vindictive, and inhuman manner, perfectly characteristic of the Yankee race, have declared quinine, opium, and other medicines necessary for the relief of suffering, the restoration of health and the salvation of life, "contraband of war"! The Yankee officers and soldiers make war upon defenceless men and helpless women and children, and the Yankee Government valiantly assails the sick and the dying!

It may be supposed that the Yankee character has now been painted in strong colors, and is complete, but such is not the case; the portrait still needs the finishing touch. In entire keeping with their invariable course of treachery and inhumanity, the base Yankees attempted to make the exchange of prisoners, into which they were finally compelled, the means of dealing us another assassin-like stab. Our soldiers in their power, who were just about to return to their homes, and to mingle once more with their comrades in arms, were driven, by their Yankee guards, into the pest-houses where their patients had died of small-pox! The Yankees, in their fiend-like malignity and constitutional cowardice, hoped by this means to introduce that loathsome disease amongst the Confederate soldiers, and thus to destroy by the plague the gallant enemies they trembled to encounter in the field. To this last extreme of baseness no savage tribe, of which I have any knowledge, has ever yet descended, even in their most barbarous wars. This lowest depth of treachery and villainy was reserved for the Yankees. The picture is now complete, and the Yankee Abolitionist stands out confessed, and in bold relief, the greatest moral monster of the world. By this last act he has crowned all his deeds of degradation, and stands alone, conspicuously pre-eminent in unapproachable infamy. The Yankees have become converts to, and have improved upon, the doctrine of the British Ministry, which was reprobated by every civilized nation, and so eloquently and emphatically denounced by the great Earl of Chatham: they have, in this war, unscrupulously "used all the means which God, and nature, and Satan, have put into their hands." Would not the innumerable atrocities committed, and the persistent violation of all laws, human and divine, by the Yankee fanatics during this war, fully justify the South in raising the black flag? Do they not even seem to require it? And this is the people who would have us renew the Union with them! These are they who dream of reconstruction! Never, never, never! Rather than this, let us have war forever – "war to the knife!" Rather than this, let our last brave defender die in our last stronghold, striking gallantly to the last for a murdered people and his ruined country. Rather than ever again have any further connection with the abhorred Yankee, in any way whatever, political or commercial, moral or religious, it were far better to resort to even a worse alternative than annihilation, and become the subjects of England or of France, or even of the most consummate despot of the most petty state in Europe. Any destiny, any fate, is preferable to subjection to, or association with, that abandoned race, whose abominations and atrocities would put to shame the bestiality of a Caligula, or the cruelty of a Nero. Although I have but little faith in it, the indications of a speedy acknowledgment of our national independence, or intervention, by the European powers, and the marked change of opinion and feeling at the North, threatening a civil conflict within the domains of Lincoln, furnish some grounds for anticipating the probability of the conclusion of peace at no very distant day; and it becomes important to consider the extent, character and terms, of that peace which the Confederate Government may with propriety, dignity and proper self-respect, consent to ratify. Here my task is greatly diminished, and my purpose anticipated, by Mr. Foote, in a series of appropriate and able joint resolutions offered by him on the 13th of January in the Congress of the Confederate States, of the use of which I gladly avail myself. The joint resolutions are as follows:

> The people of the Confederate States of America having, in the progress of the pending war, most clearly demonstrated their ability to maintain by arms the claim to separate independence, which they have heretofore asserted before the world, and being inflexibly resolved never to relinquish the struggle in which they are engaged until the great object for which they have been contending shall have been finally accomplished; in view of the fact that a great political reaction in opposition to the bloody and unnatural war now in a course of prosecution, has displayed itself in several of the most populous and influential States of what was once honorably known as "the United States of America"; and, in view of the additional fact that, even among the avowed opponents of despotism and the recognized friends of peace, in the North, a grave and deplorable misapprehension has of late arisen in re-

gard to the true condition of public sentiment in the South touching the question of reconstructing that political Union once existing under the protection of what is known as the Federal Constitution. Now, in order that no further misunderstanding of the kind referred to may hereafter prevail, and in order that the unchangeable determination of our Government and people, in reference to the terms upon which alone they would bring the sanguinary struggle to a close, may be made known, the Congress of the Confederate States of America do resolve as follows:

1. There is no plan of reconstructing what was formerly known as the federal Union, to which the people of the Confederate States will ever consent. Wrongs too grievous and multiplied have been committed upon us and upon our most cherished rights, by a *united* North, since this unprovoked and most wicked war commenced; a majority of the people of the Northern States have too evidently shown themselves to be utterly incapable of self-government, and unmindful of all the fundamental principles upon which alone republican institutions can be maintained. They have too long submitted patiently to the iron rule of the basest and most degrading despotism that the world has yet known; for too long a period of time they have openly and unblushingly sympathized with the lawless and ferocious miscreants who have been sent into the bosom of the unoffending South to spill the precious blood of our most valued citizens – to pollute and desecrate all that we hold in especial respect and veneration – to rob us of our property – to expel us from our homes, and wantonly to devastate our country – to allow even of the possibility of our ever again consenting to hold the least political connection with those who have so cruelly outraged our sensibilities and so profoundly dishonored themselves, and in association with whom we feel that we could not expect that freedom which we love, that self-respect which we are determined ever to culti-

vate, and the esteem and sympathy of civilized and Christian nations.

2. Whilst the Confederate States of America are not at all responsible for the existing war, and have been, at all times, ready to participate in such arrangements as would be best suited to bring it to a close, in a manner consistent with their own safety and honor, they could not yield their consent to an armistice of a single day or hour, so long as the incendiary proclamation of the atrocious monster now bearing rule in Washington City shall remain unrevoked; nor could the Government of said Confederate States agree to negotiate at all in regard to a suspension of hostilities except upon the basis of a formal and unconditional recognition of their independence.

3. Whenever the friends of peace in the North shall grow strong enough to constrain Abraham Lincoln and his flagitious Cabinet to withdraw said proclamation, and propose an armistice upon the basis aforesaid, the Government of the Confederate States will be ready to accede to said proposition of armistice, with a view to the settlement of all existing difficulties.

4. Should peace be at any time brought about, the Confederate States of America would freely consent to the formation of a just and mutually advantageous commercial treaty with all the States now constituting the United States, *except New England* – with whose people, and in whose ignoble love of gold, and brutifying fanaticism, this disgraceful war has mainly originated – in consideration of which facts the people of the Confederate States of America are firmly and deliberately resolved to have no intercourse whatever hereafter, either direct or indirect, political, commercial or social, under any circumstances which could be possibly imagined to exist, with said States of New England or the people therein resident.

5. The Government of the Confederate States, in

consideration of the change in public sentiment which has occurred in several of the Northern States, wherein political elections have been recently held – sympathizing most kindly with those by whose manly exertions that change has been brought about – would be willing to conclude a just and honorable peace with any one or more of said States who (renouncing all political connection with New England) may be found willing to stipulate for desisting at once from the further prosecution of the war against the South; and, in such case, the Government of the Confederate States would be willing to enter into a league, offensive and defensive, with the States thus desisting, of a permanent and enduring character.

6. The Government of the Confederate States is now willing, as it has heretofore repeatedly avowed itself to be, whenever the States bordering upon the Mississippi river, or any of them, shall have declared their inclination to withdraw from the further prosecution of the war upon the South (which, could it be successful, would only have the effect of destroying their own best market), to guarantee to them, in the most effectual and satisfactory manner, the peaceful and uninterrupted navigation of the said Mississippi river and its tributaries, and to open to them at once the markets of the South, greatly enhanced in value to them as they would be by the permanent exclusion of all articles of New England growth or manufacture.

7. The course of practical neutrality in regard to the pending war heretofore pursued by the States and Territories west of the Rocky Mountains, has afforded the highest gratification to the people of the Confederate States of America; and it is hoped that the day is not far distant when said States and Territories, consulting their own obvious safety and future welfare, will withdraw from all political connection with a Government which has, heretofore, been a source of continual oppression to

them; and when said States and Territories, asserting their separate independence, shall appropriate to themselves the manifold advantages sure to result from such a movement – among which may be reckoned, 1st. Relief from grievous and exhausting tariff regulations, now being rigidly enforced. 2d. Relief from all the discredit resulting inevitably from the prosecution of the present unjust and unauthorized war. 3d. Relief from the pressure of a despotism the most heartless and atrocious ever yet established. 4th. Relief from the crushing weight of taxation unavoidably growing out of the war. 5th. The exclusive use and enjoyment of all the rich mineral lands stretching along the slope of the Pacific. 6th. Free trade with all the nations of the earth, and a future maritime growth and power that has no parallel; and lastly, a monopoly of the trade of the Pacific Ocean.

These joint resolutions, with some alterations and additions, will embody all those essential rules and principles which, in my opinion, are absolutely necessary for the governance of the South in the conclusion of peace. The entire exclusion of New England is absolutely indispensable, but upon this point I shall have a few words to add at the end of this number.

The integrity of the territory of the States of the Confederacy must be preserved entire and perfect. Further, Maryland, should she desire it when released from her present thraldom, must be allowed to become one of the Confederate States. We should rejoice to own, as part of our country her fair territory intact, and her magnificent Bay, if such be her real wish; but if she shall prefer submission to Northern despotism to freedom and honor with the South, we can very well do without her, and God forbid that we should use any efforts to influence, far less to sway her decision! Notwithstanding the expressed opinion of Lincoln that there is no line for a division of the country, we can find one, I believe, running with the Northern boundary of Maryland and Virginia, the Ohio river, and the north line of Missouri, and thence west indefinitely. To admit any free State, or a State partly free, into our Confederacy, would be suicidal. While perfectly willing to live in entire harmony, and to conclude equitable treaties with the Northern States, we must be especially on our guard against all "entangling alliances" with them. Let them enjoy the free navigation of the Mississippi river, in its whole extent, and the immense advantages of our markets, if they will first do us justice, not only by ceasing to make war upon us, but by the repeal of all their "personal liberty bills," and all other acts of legislation hostile to the South, and guaranteeing to us, so far as rests with them, the security of our slave property. Let the owners of runaway slaves be well assured that they shall have every proper facility for, and assistance in, the capture of their absconding property, both by the people and the laws of each of the Northern and Western States with which we may establish friendly relations; and if the slave cannot be found and recovered, let the State into which he first escaped be required, as in justice it should be, to indemnify the owner for his loss. These same States should, at the same time, agree to introduce into the South no article of New England's manufacture or production, nor any kind of merchandise which has ever been, even for an hour, in one of her ports. This obligation should extend to and cover all the property of New Englanders, no matter where they are located, or where they may have established branches of their Yankee houses.

All books, periodicals, newspapers, and printed matter of every description, the production of Yankee presses, or with which any Yankee, no matter where, has had anything to do whatever, either as writer, publisher or vendor, should be as strictly excluded from the whole territory of the Confederacy as we would exclude "plague, pestilence and famine." When the Western States will promptly and cheerfully aid us in carrying out these objects, demanded by our self-respect and our security alike, then, and not till then, let them enjoy all the pleasure and the profit of friendly commercial intercourse with the Confederacy.

Towards the fanatics of New England our course should, in my view, be entirely different. As said the English, after the destruction of the Armada, "war ever, with the Spaniards," so say I, "war ever, with the Yankees!" No peace, no truce, no armistice, but open unsparing war, until these pests of society and bane of the whole human family, disabled, crushed, paralyzed, impotent for evil, are wholly confined to their own barren hills, and within their own rock-bound coast. For my own part I would willingly see them, in the language of their pet Butler, "exterminated," but this, I am well aware, is impracticable. The leviathan of the sea, the behemoth of the land, the king of the forest, may, but worthless vermin never can, be exterminated. When their annoyance becomes intolerable, they are destroyed by thousands; still thousands escape to their holes and their hiding places, and notwithstanding their noxious and noisome character, are secure in their insignificance. They are thenceforth but little heeded, and are regarded with contemptuous dislike, or scornful indifference. In that position I might cease to abhor them, but now my hatred is as deep and enduring as that of Hannibal for Rome. I would confiscate their property on land and ravage their commerce upon the sea. Even were their ships wrecked upon our coasts, their crews should be imprisoned and fined, in retaliation for their laws to fine and imprison the master who, in pursuit of his slave, entered their land of bigotry and misrule. We cannot consider them "as we do the rest of mankind, enemies in war; in peace friends," but must look upon them at all times as foes – in war avowed, in peace secret, but bitter enemies. I would strip them of their property until they had fully indemnified us for the slaves they have stolen, and paid for their luxury of the "underground railroad."

To recompense all the evils and to repay all the millions of which they have plundered us is, I know, impossible. Even if their whole barren country were brought to the hammer, and we were to blacken their bodies and sell them to the planter, as they have, themselves, blackened their souls and sold them to Satan, the whole amount would scarcely be a tithe of the immense debt contracted by their villainy. They are the people, and the only one pretending to be civilized, who realize Burke's description in his vivid picture of the character of the Hindoo idolaters who inhabited the Carnatic – "a people who would either sign no convention, or whom no covenant and no obligation could bind."

We cannot safely enter into any treaty with them, even if we would, for they have violated every obligation, and trampled upon every sanction; and like perjured men, have no security to offer for the faithful performance of their stipulations. Here, from their own follies and vices, all their boasted ingenuity fails them in morals and diplomacy, as it will again ere long, in what they regard as of vastly more importance, temporal prosperity and the acquisition of money. The markets of the South are already closed against them forever; those of the West soon will be, and in those of the rest of the world they confess their inability to compete with their European rivals. The time of a just but terrible retribution draws rapidly nigh, when, unable longer to sell their inferior goods in any market in the world, their warehouses will be closed, their manufactories will fall down piecemeal, their ships rot idle in port, and the Yankees will be reduced to that poverty they so much dread, and which they have committed so many frauds, vices and crimes to avoid. May none of them ever be naturalized, or even permitted to settle down, upon any terms, in the South. Let these bigoted, fanatical, mischief-making, would-be enlighteners, instructors, exemplars, and reformers of the moral, political and religious world, be branded, like Cain, for their crimes, and held up to the lasting scorn and derision of the world. More intolerant than the Mussulman, their war-cry has ever been, "Puritanism and tribute, or the sword!" and outraged humanity will make their infamy immortal!

They will be recorded in history, and remembered by posterity, as the Ishmaelites of Europe, the Bedouins of civilization, the Pharisees of Christendom, the disgrace of mankind, the dishonor of the Christian faith, the bane of morality – *hostis humani generis* – the curse of society, and the enemies of the human race.

www.ingramcontent.com/pod-product-compliance
Lightning Source LLC
Chambersburg PA
CBHW060259050426

42448CB00009B/1692